Advance Praise for *A Five-Mile Walk*

This is a wonderfully warm and wise guide for any Christian seeking to live our faith more fully. Michael Brown highlights the words of the Bible with practical suggestions and insightful questions about Christian living both individually and in community. No reader will be disappointed by these pages. I warmly recommend that you take them in hand and see for yourself how your journey might be more meaningful.

—*Carol M. Perry, SU*
Resident Bible Scholar
Marble Collegiate Church

In this road map to modern Christianity, Michael Brown offers an invaluable resource for individuals and communities living with the conviction that an ancient faith can and must be vibrant and transformational today. Be prepared to be changed and challenged by this excellent book.

—*Rev. Dr. Amy Butler*

Smyth & Helwys Publishing, Inc.
6316 Peake Road
Macon, Georgia 31210-3960
1-800-747-3016
©2016 by Michael B. Brown

Library of Congress Cataloging-in-Publication Data

Names: Brown, Michael B., 1949- author.
Title: A Five-mile walk : exploring themes in the experience of Christian faith
and discipleship / by Michael B. Brown.
Other titles: 5-mile walk
Description: Macon : Smyth & Helwys, 2016.
Identifiers: LCCN 2015045717 | ISBN 9781573128520 (pbk. : alk. paper)
Subjects: LCSH: Christian life. | Spiritual formation.
Classification: LCC BV4501.3 .B77155 2016 | DDC 248.4--dc23
LC record available at http://lccn.loc.gov/2015045717

MICHAEL B. BROWN

A FIVE-MILE WALK

EXPLORING THEMES

IN THE

EXPERIENCE

OF

CHRISTIAN FAITH

AND

DISCIPLESHIP

Also by Michael B. Brown

Bottom Line Beliefs
Making the Timeless Word Timely

This book is dedicated to the congregation and staff
of Marble Collegiate Church in New York City.
It is a daily blessing to make the walk of faith with them.

Special thanks to Kate Troy for her careful
attention to detail in proofing the rough draft
of this manuscript prior to its submission for publication.
—MBB

Contents

Introduction

In this book, I invite you to walk with me along five avenues that are essential to Christian faith and discipleship. Originally I entertained the ideas of calling the book either *A Five-Mile Stroll* (that sounded too easy) or *A Five-Mile March* (that sounded too exacting). The Christian journey falls somewhere between those two extremes. Sometimes it is a stroll along quiet shores. Other times it is an uphill climb on narrow, snow-covered mountain paths. Usually, it is simply a walk in the direction of wholeness, one step after another, sometimes even two steps forward and one step back.

Learning what we believe about God and what God expects from us is an ongoing journey. In this book we will consider five of the paths that journey takes. There are others, to be sure. But these five are indispensable for those who are serious about Christian faith *and* about living faithfully.

Though this is not primarily a book about psychology, we will address some of the human emotions we all experience. That is because faith and feelings always converge. We neither believe nor live in vacuums. Our experience of God and Scripture always influences (and is often influenced by) our emotions.

Though this is not a motivational-thinking book, we will address attitude. That is because in life, what we are looking for is what we usually tend to find. Look for goodness, and it can be discovered. Expect the worst, and that is usually what you will encounter. Jesus talked about people who looked at the same field. Most saw weeds, but one among them saw wheat. Attitude matters.

Though this is not solely a book about the demands of Christian living, we will address some of the expectations our faith places on us (what we often refer to as God's *calls*). When you and I were created, we were endowed with certain gifts, talents, and passions. Those endowments were not random accidents of biology or Mother Nature. Instead, they were attributes God assigned to us in order to achieve certain purposes. We are expected to make a difference in the world.

Though this is not essentially a book about ecclesiology, we will address corporate discipleship. In other words, we will consider what it means to be the church. Throughout the past two thousand years, the Christian faith has always been lived more in community than in solitude. So it is incumbent on us to ask from time to time what components are necessary (and what actions are required) to make churches healthy.

Though this is not wholly a book about a strictly personal experience of faith (flying solo as a Christian), we will address what it means internally, spiritually, and actively for a person to follow where Christ leads. Ultimately our faith always winds up confronting, comforting, calling, and challenging us as individuals.

There are five sections in the book. Each contains suggested Scripture lessons to read; these form the basis for each section. Since our theme is an exploration of Christian faith and discipleship, most (though not all) of the readings will be from the New Testament. In each section, the reader will find places to pause for reflection using a set of thought-provoking questions that can assist in study or discussion.

Given the framework (five sections with five sub-sections in each), this book can be examined in five sessions or in twenty-five. If you read it as a group, base that decision on (a) how much material you wish to tackle per session (especially allotting ample time for discussion) and (b) how many times you desire to gather. If you are reading it on your own, then you can study at your own pace.

Join with me now on a five-mile walk through faith and discipleship. May the walk bring you closer to where you wish to be.

—Michael B. Brown

Emotional Pathways

People frequently share with pastors that they are going through "a faith crisis." Almost without fail, they are also going through either a personal crisis or a significant life transition. I always remind them, "Wherever your emotions go, your faith goes with you." In using those words, I have two intentions.

First, I intend the statement as a word of *comfort*. When we are in a weakened state, everything that makes us who we are is often temporarily weakened as well. Physical fatigue, grief, a significant loss, and a host of other emotional weights that we sometimes carry make us question our faith. "I pray, I go to church, and I read the Bible, but nothing gets better. Is my faith in vain? Is my faith too weak?" These common questions do not always indicate a lack of faith; instead, they reflect a momentary lack of strength. Let us find comfort in the knowledge that being tired does not mean being faithless.

Second, I intend the statement as a word of *hope*. As Paula Gooder wrote, "Wherever we go, God is there."[1] Whenever we walk through the valley of any shadow, we do not walk alone. Jesus promised to be with us always, and inherent within that promise is strength for the journey. Often, in fact, we learn lessons through pain that cannot be learned in any other way, ultimately making our faith stronger rather than weaker.

Wherever we go, our faith goes with us. With that in mind, consider some of the human emotions with which we sometimes struggle (each set within a biblical framework).

Guilt

But God, who is rich in mercy, out of the great love with which he loved us, even when we were dead through our trespasses, made us alive together with Christ (by grace you have been saved), and raised us up with him, and made us sit with him in the heavenly places in Christ Jesus, that in the coming ages he might show the immeasurable riches of his grace in kindness toward us in Christ Jesus. For by grace you have been saved through faith; and this is not your own doing, it is the gift of God—not because of works, lest any man should boast. For we are his workmanship, created in Christ Jesus for good works, which God prepared beforehand, that we should walk in them. (Ephesians 2:4-10)

Psychologists tell us that guilt is now the highest-ranking emotion on the stress-indicator index. Apparently more people commit suicide because of unresolved guilt than because of any other emotion. Guilt is not yet, however, number one on the fear index. It seems that what people fear most of all is the experience of speaking in public. That figure actually ranks higher than the fear of dying, which means that at the average funeral, more people would rather be the corpse than the preacher! A recent survey conducted by a national association of psychological caregivers reported that ranking number two on the fear index is "the fear of being found out." Guilt is the most debilitating of all human emotions.

What do we do with this debilitating emotion? How do we handle it so that in the end it does not handle us?

First, it should be noted that *guilt can be a positive force.* There is a difference between confessing guilt and feeling guilty.

I took my automobile to a mechanic some time ago because it had a clicking sound under the hood. As the car's speed accelerated, the noise grew quieter until, after reaching highway speed, it went away altogether. Nonetheless, an automobile is not supposed to go "clunk, clunk, clunk" when traveling under sixty-five miles per hour. I took it to a local garage. The mechanic decided to test-drive it in order to hear the noise for himself.

That seemed like a reasonable idea, except that this particular man accelerated from 0 to 100 miles per hour in about a millisecond. It was my first occasion of experiencing the sort of G-force that astronauts report. I have to admit that it was rather intriguing, if a bit disturbing, to feel my entire body pinned to a car seat. It was like riding with Dale Earnhardt, Jr. Upon our return to the garage, the mechanic said rather nonchalantly, "I didn't hear any noise." "I don't want to seem rude," I replied, "but perhaps you didn't hear any noise because we were traveling faster than the speed of sound!" In any event, a second mechanic took it for a spin at mere mortal speed, and he heard the noise. He told me what it was and what would be involved in repairing it. Then he said, "Engine noises are warning signs. Never ignore them. They tell us that something has gone wrong that needs to be made right." Without knowing or intending it, he was speaking both psychologically and theologically.

When you feel guilt, listen to it. Examine it. Try to find out what the feeling is telling you. Then do whatever needs to be done to repair the engine and move on. Many of us fail to move on, and thus imprison ourselves. Experiencing guilt, we allow it to hold us captive. We're much like the prodigal son who returned home, beating himself up and lamenting, "Father, I am no longer worthy to be called your child." What action did the father (a character symbolizing God) take in that story? He threw open his arms, welcomed the boy back home, and said, "You, my child, are alive again. Let's have a party!" (See Luke 15:11-32.)

Guilt is not a condemnation of you as a person. Rather, it is a noise in the engine telling you that something has gone wrong that needs to be made right. Once you have dealt with it, let it go. Think of guilt as an internal professor. It is like going into a classroom and being taught. But remember that, in time, every class is completed and the students move forward. As a friend of mine used to say, there is no reason for you to remember with guilt that which God has chosen to forget. If you feel guilt, listen to it. Learn from it. Then let it go, and move forward.

Second, *Christianity is about grace.* Christ is about grace. The cross is about grace. In fact, the central and fundamental theme of the entire New Testament is grace.

You have never done anything wicked enough, low enough, or immoral enough that God is not able and willing to forgive it. Your power to sin is not as strong as God's power to forgive. Paul wrote, "By grace you have been saved through faith, and this is not your own doing lest anyone should boast. It is a gift from God" (Eph 2:8).

An old man lived alone in Ireland. The season of the year came to dig up his potato garden, which was hard work. And it was work he had to do alone, as his only son (who ordinarily would have helped him) was confined to prison for bank robbery. The father wrote a letter to his son and mentioned his predicament. Shortly thereafter, he received this reply: "For heaven's sake, Dad, do not dig up that garden! It's where I hid the money." At 4 o'clock the next morning, a team of policemen arrived and dug up the entire garden, but they did not find a single penny. Confused, the old man wrote another letter to his son, telling him what had happened and asking what he should do next. The son wrote back, "What you need to do next is plant the potatoes. Getting the garden dug up for you was the best I could accomplish from here!"

Into our experiences of sin and guilt, our senses of flaws or failures, God sends the Messiah with grace and open arms and forgiveness and fresh starts and second chances. And he says, "It's the best I can accomplish from here. Now let go of the guilt. I dug it up. It's gone. It's time for you to plant the potatoes, time for you to build a new life in which the old guilt is no longer present." The past is past. Let it go. You cannot change a single thing you ever did or failed to do. Guilt can bar you from planting new potatoes, from building a new life in a new way, which is what God desires for you. And that means that guilt is not simply a punishment you inflict on yourself; it is also an act of defiance against God, refusing to live the life God wants you to live. Let it go.

A beautiful adage says, "Whoever falls from God's right hand is caught into his left." What an empowering thought, and it is all about God's love and grace.

Many years ago, a story appeared in the national news about a nine-year-old boy on a baseball sandlot behind the apartment where he lived in a small California town. I clipped the article from the paper and still have it in a file somewhere. The story said that the child was playing right field. That's where young children play when they cannot catch the ball well (because children hit fewer balls to right field than to any other place in a ballpark). His teammates put him there so they wouldn't have to worry about his dropping too many balls that were hit his way. His two-year-old sister stood on the kitchen table in their second-floor apartment, watching the big kids play and wishing they would let her join their game. She pressed her face against the screen, watching, until the screen began to protrude. Her brother in right field saw what was happening. He yelled at her to get back, but she did not get back, and the screen popped out. The little girl fell through the air, turning a complete somersault on her way toward the ground. Meanwhile, her brother ran to a spot beneath the window, held out his arms, caught her, and held on. He then carried her back up to the apartment with nothing but a scratch on her forehead to show for the adventure. A local reporter heard of the incident, talked to the little boy, and printed it in the hometown newspaper. The Associated Press later picked up the story (which is how I came to read it). The reporter asked the child, "Weren't you afraid when your sister fell?" "I was for a minute," the boy answered, "'cause I ain't too good at catching!" But he did catch her, and carried her back to where she was meant to be.

"Whoever falls from God's right hand is caught into his left." Therein lies the cure for guilt. God loves us not because we deserve it but because we need it. Even more deeply, God loves us simply because we are God's children. Whenever we fall in whatever way(s), God is there to catch us and carry us back to where we were meant to be. All we have to do is trust and surrender to the unseen arms outstretched beneath us. That is precisely what Paul meant when he wrote, "While we were yet sinners, Christ died for us" (Rom 5:8). "While we were yet sinners" (broken, unworthy), God's love for us has remained constant.

What do we do about guilt? There are really two choices. Either we allow it to imprison us, debilitate us, and wreck our lives, *or* we listen to it, learn from it, and then hand it over to God and let it go. Grace is God's act of digging the garden. We are asked to accept the gift, plant the seeds of a new life, and allow them to grow. When we wallow in guilt and self-deprecation, we are literally saying, "My power to sin is stronger than God's power to forgive." Honestly, who could be foolish enough to believe something like that? Hear Paul's words again: "By grace you have been saved through faith, and this is not your own doing lest anyone should boast. It is a gift from God" (Eph 2:8).

Reflection

1. Identify ways in which guilt can be a debilitating emotion.

_____

_____

_____

_____

2. Identify ways in which guilt can lead to healing or resolution.

_____

_____

_____

_____

3. What steps can be taken to receive forgiveness from someone whom we have offended? Are there steps that must be taken to receive forgiveness from God?

_____

_____

_____

_____

Loneliness

Then Jesus went with them to a place called Gethsemane, and he said to his disciples, "Sit here, while I go yonder and pray." And taking with him Peter and the two sons of Zebedee, he began to be sorrowful and troubled. Then he said to them, "My soul is very sorrowful, even to death; remain here, and watch with me." And going a little farther he fell on his face and prayed, "My Father, if it be possible, let this cup pass from me; nevertheless, not as I will, but as thou wilt." And he came to the disciples and found them sleeping; and he said to Peter, "So, could you not watch with me one hour? Watch and pray that you may not enter into temptation; the spirit indeed is willing, but the flesh is weak." Again, for the second time, he went away and prayed, "My Father, if this cannot pass unless I drink it, thy will be done." And again he came and found them sleeping, for their eyes were heavy. So, leaving them again, he went away and prayed for the third time, saying the same words. Then he came to the disciples and said to them, "Are you still sleeping and taking your rest? Behold, the hour is at hand, and the Son of man is betrayed into the hands of sinners. Rise, let us be going; see, my betrayer is at hand." (Matthew 26:36-46)

A friend of mine served as a chaplain at a Veterans Administration hospital in the mountains of North Carolina. He has an endless supply of stories from that work, some funny, some tragic, and many inspiring. Let me share one of the latter. He said a certain survivor of the Vietnam War was occasionally a patient in that facility. The man had lost both legs in a minefield. He came back to the States and completed his education, earned a doctoral degree, and worked successfully as a college administrator. But from time to time complications arose from his amputations, and he wound up in the hospital for a few days or even weeks. On one occasion, my chaplain friend was talking with the man and made the remark, "You know, I am impressed by all that you've accomplished from a wheelchair." The gentleman in the chair replied, "I lost part of my body but I kept all of my soul."

In that statement, he articulated a basic, bottom-line desire in life: the desire to be made whole. The New Testament's word for "salvation" is *soteria*. Literally translated, it means "wholeness." Our dream, inherited from biblical ancestors, is that amid the brokenness of this world (amid the brokenness of our daily lives) we can somehow become whole.

Psychologists report that loneliness is epidemic. Three out of every four American adults claim to feel lonely. They may be married or partnered with families, they may live in busy neighborhoods or crowded apartment buildings, they may work in malls surrounded by seas of other people, but still they confess a feeling of isolation, sometimes even abandonment, as if no one understands and maybe, just maybe, no one even cares. They feel lonely, and to feel lonely is to feel especially broken.

It is, of course, important to distinguish the difference between being lonely and being alone. Jesus chose to be alone on numerous occasions. More than once, we read that he "withdrew by himself to a lonely place" (ex., Matt 14:13; Luke 22:41; John 6:15). Note that the place was lonely, but Jesus was not. We are all familiar with those moments—times when you silence the phone and lock the door to your room, honestly hoping that ESPN or Netflix or a good book or Calgon can take you away from the noise, from the conversations, and from the demands of the world outside. It is not only understandable but also critical that from time to time we find a way to be alone. That, however, is a far cry from being lonely.

Jesus knew about being alone by choice, but he also knew about being lonely even when surrounded by other people. When he preached to a packed house in his hometown of Nazareth and the listeners tried to murder him for what he said, Jesus must have felt desperately lonely. On Palm Sunday, Jerusalem's streets were probably crowded with what seemed to be more people than had ever gathered along those roads before, but Jesus knew how fickle their gestures of welcome would be, and how by the week's end some would be shouting, "Crucify him!" In that moment, armed with that knowledge, he must've felt lonely. He knew in the Upper Room that one of the Twelve would betray him and another would deny him. Thus, even as they ate together and the disciples pledged their loyalty and unfailing love, it is likely that Jesus felt lonely. In the Garden of Gethsemane when Christ prayed before his arrest, the handwriting was on the wall. He knew what was coming. So he took his three most trusted friends (Peter, James, and John) to be with him. But, as it turned out, they were not essentially "with him" at all. Yes, they were nearby in the garden, but as Jesus prayed "in agony" and "his sweat fell to the ground like great drops of blood" (as he faced the reality of the cross that awaited him), they were not really *with* him. Instead, they kept falling asleep. Jesus, though in the presence of others, no doubt felt lonely. Waking them, he asked one of the loneliest questions found anywhere in the Bible: "Could you not watch with me for one hour?"

"Could you not stay close? Could you not tune in to my life and my pain? Could you not care for me and pray for me and weep with me? Could you not enter into this moment with me to spare me the agony of loneliness?" Jesus knew what it was like to be alone. He also knew what it was like to be lonely, even when surrounded by other people.

We know how that feels, too, don't we?

To be misunderstood. Abandoned. Ignored. Rejected. Forgotten. In pain when no one seems to notice or care. Frightened with no one to turn to. Always letting others lean on us, but there's no one out there for us to lean on when our weary days come.

At any given moment, more than 70 percent of us know exactly how loneliness feels, even in the midst of a crowd.

When Christ's loneliest experiences came (and none were more intense than that Thursday night when he left the Upper Room and went to Gethsemane to prepare himself to face a cross), a handful of decisions on his part seem to have made his loneliness at least bearable.

For example, *Jesus chose to be with people.* He prepared the Passover meal and ate it with his disciples. When he went to Gethsemane, he took some of those same disciples with him. And when he ventured deeper into the garden, he asked Peter, James, and John to remain near, saying to them, "Watch with me . . . and pray." Jesus knew that cultivating relationships, reaching out to others, and never cutting ourselves off from the crowd are the best antidotes we have for loneliness. He chose to be with people.

Years ago I knew a single mom who was a very deep and dear person. She struggled frequently with loneliness. Some nights when her children were with their father, she would arrive at our house unannounced around bedtime. She had a standing invitation and knew she did not have to phone. She would just show up and make her way to an empty bedroom. Often she did not even pause for conversation. She would simply say, "Tonight I could not face sleeping in that house alone." When the pain of loneliness was overbearing, she chose to be with people.

She made a good point. We can wish for friends, hope for relationships, and long for intimacy, but at some point we have to take action in order to attain that for which we yearn. Do something. Reach out to somebody. Put yourself in a place where you can reasonably expect to meet other people. If friends are "the chocolate chips of life," then at some point we have to be willing to reach into the cookie jar to find them.

When loneliness began to creep in, Jesus chose to be with people. He sought them, loved them, laughed with them, wept with them, held them close to his heart, and thus did not feel so alone.

Second, *Jesus chose to be for people.* His life, ministry, and journey to the cross were clearly neither recreational, self-centered, nor self-oriented. The traditional Christian doctrine of the atonement teaches that Jesus not only lived but also died on behalf of others. Here's how Jesus himself put it: "The Son of Man came not to be served but to serve, and to give his life as a ransom for many" (Matt 20:28).

A proven treatment for loneliness is to turn one's energies outward instead of inward, to devote one's self to the service of others, to volunteer in church, to work on a house-building project, to tutor a child, or to assist at a local service agency. The point is simply that the more we give to others, the more we get back for ourselves.

A couple had been married for fifty years. The church where they belonged decided to honor them with an anniversary reception. During the reception, the pastor asked the couple to step forward and address the crowd. The wife had grown somewhat hard of hearing and had unfortunately left her hearing aids at home. Her husband addressed the group of well-wishers and said, "My wife and I have been together fifty years, and she's always been tried and true." His wife leaned over and asked, "What did you say?" He repeated it a little more loudly: "I said you have always been tried and true." Her face turned red, and she answered, "Well, I'm tired of you, too!"

One of the best antidotes for loneliness is to be "tried and true" in our service to others—to be present for them in their times of need, to be more interested in listening than in pontificating, to be more sympathetic than judgmental, to be more compassionate than didactic, to be someone people know they can count on through thick and thin. When others know that we're there for them, usually they will also be there for us. Furthermore, to lose ourselves in the service of others who hurt is literally to *lose ourselves,* momentarily at least to lose touch with our own loneliness and pain. When we're busy helping someone else who hurts, we have less time to focus on how much we are hurting. Jesus chose to be for people.

When loneliness crept in, Jesus chose to be with others, for others, and last of all, *he chose to be with God.* "He said to Peter, James, and John,

'Remain here, and watch with me.' Then, going on a little farther, he fell on his face and prayed." Jesus understood that whereas we may feel lonely, in truth we are never really alone. God is ever near, ever loving, ever accessible to anyone who cries out in prayer.

An aging widow who shared a hillside cabin with her dog deep in the beautiful Appalachian Mountains talked with me one day about living alone. I asked, "How do you combat the loneliness?" She answered, "Sometimes at night when I sit in the house, I read the Bible. Often when I work in the garden, I pray. And in those moments, I can feel the embrace of unseen arms."

"Then, going on a little farther, Jesus fell on his face and prayed." He knew that though we may sometimes feel lonely, in truth we are never alone. Through prayer we feel the embrace of unseen arms.

Loneliness comes to everyone from time to time. It truly is unavoidable. But there are measures we can take to address it and keep living. When moments of loneliness occurred for Jesus, he chose to be (1) with people, (2) for people, and (3) with God.

Reflection

1. What is the difference between being alone and being lonely?

_____

_____

_____

_____

_____

2. How can you identify loneliness in another person? What are the most helpful ways to respond?

_____

_____

_____

_____

_____

3. What lessons can we learn from our own experiences of loneliness?

_____

_____

_____

_____

The Blues

He found him in a desert land,
and in the howling waste of the wilderness;
he encircled him, he cared for him,
he kept him as the apple of his eye.
Like an eagle that stirs up its nest,
that flutters over its young,
spreading out its wings, catching them,
bearing them on its pinions,
the LORD alone did lead him . . . (Deuteronomy 32:10-12a)

Rejoice in the Lord always; again I will say, Rejoice. Let all men
know your forbearance. The Lord is at hand. Have no anxiety about
anything, but in everything by prayer and supplication with thanks-
giving let your requests be made known to God. And the peace of God,
which passes all understanding, will keep your hearts and your minds
in Christ Jesus. Finally, brethren, whatever is true, whatever is honor-
able, whatever is just, whatever is pure, whatever is lovely, whatever is
gracious, if there is any excellence, if there is anything worthy of praise,
think about these things. (Philippians 4:4-8)

At a recent gala for The Protestant Welfare Agencies of New York, I was
introduced to a man who mentioned the signboard on Fifth Avenue in
front of our sanctuary. He said, "I pass by your church every day. One day
I plan to stop in. But I have a question. I noticed your sermon this week is
about depression. Tell me, are you going to preach about 'real' depression
or just 'sort of' depression?" I understood what he meant and reminded
him that the title ("Beating the Blues") implied that the sermon would not
be a medical explanation of clinical depression. What he called "real depression" (i.e., "clinical depression") is a chemical condition like diabetes or
hypothyroidism that requires a specific kind of attention. If a person has a
clinical condition, they need to consult a counselor for therapy *and* a good
doctor who can prescribe one of a plethora of medications on the market

nowadays that can help those with clinical depression recover emotional balance and find meaning and joy. If you have a chemical condition, you can't attend church, hear a twenty-minute sermon, and then go home well.

That being said, one-third of us at any given moment, if we were honest, would say, "I've been feeling a little down lately. I'm tired, kind of lonely, and not as happy as I used to be. I guess I sort of have the blues." All of us feel that way from time to time. It's not chemical as much as emotional, even spiritual. And our faith offers helpful and hopeful advice to assist us in coping with that kind of depression.

For those going through emotional down cycles, two passages from Hebrew Scriptures and from the Epistles extol the virtues of maintaining a *positive attitude* and *a confident faith.*

I read an article in a medical journal recently that listed ten therapies for depression. It was neither a religious journal nor a self-help guide; it was a clinical psychiatric publication. The first suggested protocol of treatment was medication. But the second treatment on the list was Cognitive Therapy. Basically, that means you can change the way you feel if you learn to change the way you think. A medical article said that clients who feel negatively must be taught to think positively. Paul said that very thing two thousand years ago: "Whatever is true, whatever is noble, whatever is right, whatever is pure, whatever is lovely, whatever is admirable, think on these things, and the peace of God will guard your hearts and your minds in Christ Jesus."

When I accepted the invitation to become Senior Minister of Marble Collegiate Church, a long-time acquaintance in the ministry said to me, "You don't really believe all that positive-thinking stuff, do you?" Let me put his remark in context. I'm not sure he's ever had a positive thought in his entire life. Behind his back, friends have two nicknames for him. In fact, they never refer to him by his real name at all. People who know him always call him either "Eeyore" (the down-in-the-mouth donkey from *Winnie-the-Pooh*) or "Dr. Doom." If either of those names comes up in a conversation, you don't need to ask who is meant by them. The guy sees every glass half empty. He's miserable, and he longs for everyone else to "go and do likewise." If you tell him about your vegetable garden, he'll start talking about beetles. If you mention you have a new puppy, he'll launch into a lecture on the high costs of vet bills. Take him to a five-star restaurant, and he'll swear his fork has a smudge on it. I have no idea why he is like that and why at some point he decided to look for the worst in life. I simply know that if the worst is what you look for, it's almost always what you're going to find.

And he finds it every day. In every church he serves, in every relationship, in every silver cloud that he's sure must have a dark lining somewhere. "Two men looked out from prison bars, One saw the mud, the other, stars."[2]

An adviser said to President Lincoln, "It's a terrible day, Mr. President," to which Lincoln replied, "We usually find the sort of day we're looking for." That's true. In this life, most of the time what we decide to seek is what we ultimately discover. That's why I told the man who denigrated hopeful, positive perspectives, "Yes, I do believe in that positive-thinking stuff. And I not only believe in it but I need it. In a world like this, I need a positive perspective in order to make it from one day to the next." Paul understood that, and he practiced it and preached it. That's why he told the Philippians to look for whatever is lovely, whatever is admirable, and to think on these things. Do that, he said, and the peace of God will fill your hearts and minds.

Life comes to all of us with pretty much the same conditions and circumstances. They vary somewhat from person to person, but if we live long enough we all have joys and sorrows, victories and defeats, triumphs and tragedies, highs and lows, good times and other times not so good. Life happens! And the difference between being basically up or usually down is not ordinarily as much about life as about how I choose to look at life. What's my focus, my perspective? Do I even give the old clichés a chance?

- "Never give up!"
- "Broken crayons still color."
- "Caterpillar today, butterfly tomorrow."
- "If at first you don't succeed, try, try again."

It's like the story of the woman on the eve of her seventh wedding who said, "I still believe there are good men are out there, even if finding one is like nailing Jell-O to a tree!"

So what about all those clichés, what about a positive attitude, what about believing the best and maintaining hope-filled spirits and perspectives? Are those attitudes no more than wishful thinking? Trying to be like Pollyanna, the little girl who always saw the good in life? A denial of reality? Or is it possible that Cognitive Therapy makes sense, that often what we think actually is what we become? Therefore, if I want a positive life, I need to think positively. If I want to succeed, I need to ignore the voices that tell me I can't. Thank goodness Bob Dylan did not listen to a music critic who said he should write for others but never record because he didn't have the voice for it. Thank goodness Fred Astaire persevered even after the assessment on one of his early auditions: "Can't sing, can't act, can dance a little." Maybe, if I want to beat the blues, it's not a bad idea to listen to Paul: "Whatever is lovely, whatever is admirable, think on these things, and the peace of God will fill your hearts and minds."

In my own low moments, I have found that in addition to prayer I can do either of three things, and most of the time they get me out of the dumps. (1) I can watch comedy (funny movies or television reruns of shows like *Everybody Loves Raymond*, *Curb Your Enthusiasm*, and *The Big Bang Theory*). (2) I can listen to upbeat music by artists like the Drifters, the Isley Brothers, Martha and the Vandelas, or Jimmy Buffett. (3) I can look at photographs that bring me joy (my wife, my children, church events, places or things that I love). I feed my mind with happy sounds and lovely images and, by doing so long enough, I am lifted up when I was down. Those things help me beat the blues. "Whatever is lovely, whatever is admirable, think on these things," Paul said, "and the peace of God will fill your hearts and minds."

When we get down in the dumps, it helps to think positively and also to *believe confidently.*

The author of Deuteronomy wrote of feeling like we're "in a desert land . . . in a barren and howling waste." That's what depression feels like. But the writer went on, saying that in that very place, "God shields us and cares for us . . . like an eagle that hovers over its young" (Deut 32:10-11).

The late brilliant Catholic priest and spiritual author, Henri Nouwen, often taught that depression (not clinical, but rather "having the blues") is ordinarily the result of opinion—someone else's opinion of me or my opinion of myself. If others say I'm not good enough, or if down deep I think I'm not good enough; if others reject me or ignore me or belittle me, or if I do not learn to accept and affirm myself for who I am; if others say that I am unworthy, or if I basically feel unworthy, that results in depression. It results in feeling, as the writer of Deuteronomy puts it, like I am a stranger "in a desert land . . . in a barren and howling waste." If, in fact, depression is the result of someone's opinion, then the answer to that is to confront opinion with Truth. Nouwen's indispensable truth is that we are God's beloved,[3] and that is the only opinion that actually matters. What God said of Jesus at his baptism is what God says of you and me: "This is my beloved child, with whom I am well pleased."

That is God's opinion about you. It doesn't matter what anyone else has ever said. It doesn't even matter if you feel unworthy. God's opinion trumps all the others. You are the apple of God's eye. Your picture is on God's mantle. And whenever angels drop in for a visit, God shows them that picture and says, "This is my beloved child, with whom I am well pleased." Nouwen was right. It's hard to keep feeling low when we know that God's love for us is so high.

Reflection

1. What things create a sense of sadness within me?

_____

_____

_____

_____

2. What do my sources of sadness indicate about me?

_____

_____

_____

_____

3. Does my faith help me beat the blues? If "Yes," explain.

_____

_____

_____

_____

Grief

Now if Christ is preached as raised from the dead, how can some of you say that there is no resurrection of the dead? But if there is no resurrection of the dead, then Christ has not been raised; if Christ has not been raised, then our preaching is in vain and your faith is in vain. We are even found to be misrepresenting God, because we testified of God that he raised Christ, whom he did not raise if it is true that the dead are not raised. For if the dead are not raised, then Christ has not been raised. If Christ has not been raised, your faith is futile and you are still in your sins. Then those also who have fallen asleep in Christ have perished. If for this life only we have hoped in Christ, we are of all men most to be pitied . . . .

Lo! I tell you a mystery. We shall not all sleep, but we shall all be changed, in a moment, in the twinkling of an eye, at the last trumpet. For the trumpet will sound, and the dead will be raised imperishable, and we shall be changed. For this perishable nature must put on the imperishable, and this mortal nature must put on immortality. When the perishable puts on the imperishable, and the mortal puts on immortality, then shall come to pass the saying that is written:

"Death is swallowed up in victory."
"O death, where is thy victory?
O death, where is thy sting?"

The sting of death is sin, and the power of sin is the law. But thanks be to God, who gives us the victory through our Lord Jesus Christ. (1 Corinthians 15:12-19, 51-57)

I am neither a nihilist nor a pessimist. For heaven's sake, I am pastor of America's home of Positive Thinking. Dr. Peale would come back to haunt me if I were someone who focuses on the shadowy side of life. I am, however, a realist. And as such, I have a theory about life. Here it is: *Life is not the last five minutes of the movie.* For the first hour and twenty-five minutes of the movie, there may have been problems and foul-ups galore, but in the last five minutes somehow Tom Hanks and Meg Ryan always got together. The real world is rarely so neat or happily-ever-after.

Almost everyone who saw it marveled at the extraordinary acting and exceptional story in the film *On Golden Pond.* As you recall, in the last five minutes of that movie Henry Fonda is helping Katharine Hepburn (who plays his wife) move a box of her mother's china. Fonda's character has just turned eighty and has health problems. Suddenly he drops the box, clutches his chest, and falls on the porch. Hepburn races for his nitroglycerin pills. Then she begs God not to take her husband. "You don't want him, God," she pleads. "He's just an old fool!" And then, right on cue, the Hollywood miracle occurs. Both Fonda and Hepburn realize that he simply strained a muscle lifting the box of china. He's fine. He gets up, dusts himself off, and the two of them walk hand-in-hand to stand on the pier and watch the sun glimmer on Golden Pond. Such were the last five minutes of a wonderful movie.

However, in reality, both Fonda and Hepburn are gone now. In the end, no scriptwriter could change that for them. Life, real life, is rarely like the last five minutes of the movie.

Deep down, we all understand that. Consider the actual titles of some best-selling books from the not-too-distant past: *Stiff (The Curious Lives Of Cadavers), Plague Pox, Toxic Psychiatry*, and one of my favorites, Elizabeth Wurtzel's book *Prozac Nation* (popular enough to have been adapted into a movie). We know that life is anything but a Hollywood fairytale.

Paul knew that, too. He provided a laundry list of problems he had experienced in his own life: being shipwrecked, adrift at sea, without food, falsely accused and imprisoned, and three times flogged almost to death. When it came down to the last five minutes of his movie, there was no magical deliverance from suffering. Instead, he was convicted of the crime of preaching Christ and was sentenced to die. Paul knew that life is not always fair.

While browsing through a Barnes and Noble store, I ran across a coffee table book, a collection of cartoons that had appeared in *The New Yorker* magazine. All of the cartoons were about dogs. On the back cover was one of the cartoons, a picture of two dogs sitting in a backyard talking with one another. One dog says to the other, "I bit a human once. They taste just like chicken." The book is titled *Scotch and Toilet Water.* What a great book title! It states right on the cover that life is not like the last five minutes of a happy movie. It is instead a mixture of good and bad, joy and sorrow, love and loss, "Scotch and toilet water." Life, says *The New Yorker* and the Bible, is not always fair.

Good people get sick.

Young people become addicts.

Babies go hungry, while a derelict dies of malnutrition in a skid row tenement with $90,000 hidden away in his mattress.

One hundred and thirty thousand youth and children sleep beneath America's bridges every night, while the news carries a story of a family not far from my city that recently completed construction of their $200 million new home.

There are "wars and rumors of wars" (Matt 24:6).

The very young and the very old and the very vulnerable are regularly victimized.

The sex-for-sale industry has created a new global culture of slavery with eight hundred thousand new victims (mostly girls at the average age of fourteen, some as young as five) being bought and sold every year.

Boko Haram, rather than bringing our girls back, sells them to wealthy, decadent men who dehumanize them for personal gratification.

ISIS beheads the innocent on YouTube, performing godless atrocities in the name of a God they obviously do not know.

In the land of Jesus' birth, children in some places are afraid to walk to school.

In the city of Jesus' birth, residents are virtually imprisoned within a wall imposed around them.

Good and innocent people suffer from everything from Ebola to AIDS, and most do not have the financial wherewithal to protect their lives or the lives of their families.

Added to that, of course, is the matter of death, the cruelest of all life's tragedies. You stand beside a grave and weep bitter tears, you watch your loved ones with their breaking hearts, you say "good-bye" to someone who is absolutely irreplaceable, you struggle to remember the sound of a voice as it called your name, and there is no scriptwriter around who can change it all and create a happy ending. In those bitter moments, how does one find the strength to keep on keeping on?

Paul asked the same question. "If we have hope in this life only," he wrote—if this life is all there is, if ultimately our lives are nothing more than momentary blips on some cosmic screen, if it is truly "ashes to ashes and dust to dust" and nothing more—"then we of all people are most to be pitied."

But, Paul continued, this life is not all there is. "Behold, I tell you a mystery . . . we shall all be changed, in a moment, in the twinkling of an eye." Certainly Paul used those words to describe the literal change from physical to eternal life for those who die, but the words are also pertinent for those who grieve. There you stand, damp with tears, feeling empty and numb, wondering how the world can go on as if nothing happened, when suddenly, unexpectedly, "in the twinkling of an eye," something happens to bring comfort.

It may be a card or a phone call. It may be remembering a hymn or a Scripture verse from your childhood. It may be a photograph you find or something a loved one says or does just when you need it most. It may be an unexpected act of kindness from a friend or stranger. But suddenly, "in the twinkling of an eye," your sadness is interrupted by mercy.

The week after my father died, a family in the church I was serving was gracious enough to let me use their place at the beach to rest, relax, reflect, and regroup. One day I went to lunch in Wilmington, North Carolina, a beautiful city where the Neuse River flows into the Atlantic Ocean. I was standing alone in a buffet line, waiting to reach the food, head hung low, having a hard time dealing with the memories of my dad who would have enjoyed being there with me. Suddenly I heard a little voice, like an angel's, which maybe she was. "Hi, my name is Alicia. I'm three. What's your name?" Before me stood a beautiful three-year-old child with braided hair and large eyes, sweetly smiling up at me. She walked over without invitation, hugged my leg, and then extended her arms for me to pick her up. Her mom nodded that it was okay, so I did. Little Alicia softly nuzzled her head on my shoulder. I stood there and hugged her, remembering when I used to hold my children that way and how good it felt, even remembering being held in my own dad's arms.

Her mother, almost apologetically, said, "Sometimes she's too friendly. Alicia, you need to get down." I mouthed the words (so that the child could not hear but her mother could understand): "My father died last week. I need this hug." So her mom kindly waited and smiled as a three-year-old child surprised a grieving stranger with the gift of love. I believe God hugged me through Alicia.

Most of us have been there. Sometimes, "in a moment, in the twinkling of an eye," something unexpected happens in the midst of your grief (most of the time that something is someone), and you feel God's hug.

But there is something else that brings us comfort. It is a whisper of faith, a hope that life at the end is not merely extinguished. For "if we have hope in this life only, then we of all people are most to be pitied." Paul believed and taught that the resurrection of Christ meant that all God's children can count on that same resurrection: "For the trumpet will sound, and the dead will be raised incorruptible, so that death is swallowed up in victory. O Death, where is your sting? O Death, where is your victory? Thanks be to God, who has given us the victory through our Lord Jesus Christ!"

The book *A Man Called Peter* was Catherine Marshall's biography of her husband, the famous minister and chaplain to the US Senate. Recalling his unexpected death, she wrote of how Peter was lying on a stretcher, being carried to an ambulance in the process of dying, and through his pain he whispered these final words to his wife: "Darling, I'll see you in the morning." In the dark months following, she wrote that it was his unshakable faith in a new morning where life goes on forever that gave her the strength to survive his death. And later, it was the memory of the faith he had always preached (especially faith in a God of comfort who will not let us grieve alone) that helped her heal.[4]

And so, to all who have suffered the loss of loved ones, to family members who have wept bitter tears, there remains a word of comfort straight from the heart of the Christian faith: (1) Life does not end at the funeral. Instead, for those whom we have loved and lost, life that is endless begins there. Jesus said so himself: "And I, if I be lifted up, will draw all others unto myself" (John 12:32). (2) Our loved ones, in their living and in their loving, left us lessons for our lives. When we remember those lessons and replicate them, our loved ones stay alive through us. And (3) the God who has received their spirits to be with him in heaven will also send the Spirit to be with us in our grief.

My father used to quote William Cullen Bryant's poem, "Ode to a Waterfowl." How beautifully the poem articulated Christian faith in the face of grief:

> Thou'rt gone! The abyss of heaven
> Hath swallowed up thy form; yet on my heart
> Deeply hath sunk the lesson thou has given,
> And shall not soon depart.
> He who, from zone to zone,
> Guides through the boundless sky their certain flight,
> In the long way that I must tread alone
> Will lead my steps aright.[5]

Reflection

1. Whom have you lost, and how do you remember that person?

_____

_____

_____

_____

2. How does God help you through grief?

_____

_____

_____

_____

3. Psychologists tell us there are five stages of grief:

• Shock ("This can't be true.")
• Denial ("This doesn't seem real.")
• Anger ("This is not fair.")
• Guilt ("If only I had [or hadn't] . . . .")
• Resolution and Recovery ("I am learning to discover a new normal.")

How is the Christian faith experienced or expressed in each of those five stages?

_____

_____

_____

_____

Surviving the Storms

(This chapter is a sermon I preached at Marble Collegiate Church in New York City on Sunday, November 4, 2012, immediately following the devastation caused in our area by Hurricane Sandy. Study questions are included at the conclusion.)

> *On that day, when evening had come, he said to them, "Let us go across to the other side." And leaving the crowd, they took him with them in the boat, just as he was. And other boats were with him. And a great storm of wind arose, and the waves beat into the boat, so that the boat was already filling. But he was in the stern, asleep on the cushion; and they woke him and said to him, "Teacher, do you not care if we perish?" And he awoke and rebuked the wind, and said to the sea, "Peace! Be still!" And the wind ceased, and there was a great calm. He said to them, "Why are you afraid? Have you no faith?" And they were filled with awe, and said to one another, "Who then is this, that even wind and sea obey him?" (Mark 4:35-41)*

A week ago we thought we would be listening to Dr. Anna Carter Florence right now, preaching a stirring sermon for All Saints Sunday. However, last Sunday we did not know that we would experience a crisis of unprecedented proportion this week. So today it made more sense for us to gather as family. We will entertain guests later, and Anna will be back with us (hopefully soon). For today, however, as I said, we need to be together as family . . . to process . . . and pray . . . and just love one another.

I'm not going to recount what you already know, what you have seen on TV, read in the news, or lived through. We all witnessed the Jersey shore that was washed away, the fires in Breezy Point, the waters filling our subways and PATH, the homes destroyed on Staten Island and Long Island, the businesses swallowed up at Coney Island and Battery Park, the dangling crane, the fears, the tears, the enormity of it all. But, as your pastor, there are four simple observations I want to make this morning.

We survived. Admittedly, for a while Monday night it felt like the storm would win. The disciples felt the same way in our morning lesson. They thought they were going to die: "Teacher, do you not care if we perish?" They thought the storm would kill them, but it didn't. And it didn't kill us, either. Marble Collegiate Church is still standing here, as it has on this corner since 1854. And you and I are still sitting inside it, a little the worse for wear, but present and alive.

Mayor Bloomberg was correct when he observed that this storm was the strongest we've ever seen in this city, but New Yorkers are stronger than the hurricane was! And the same can be said, of course, for our neighbors in Connecticut and New Jersey and as far south as the West Virginia mountains and the Carolinas' shores.

You folks lived through 9/11. You will live through a hurricane. And whatever other storms our city, or our church, or we as individuals face in the future, somehow we will be given sufficient strength to endure.

Recently my wife and I were on the second worst airline flight I have ever experienced. Our plane was bounced around like a basketball. During one of the rockiest moments, Page reached over and grasped my arm (with sufficient strength to cut off anyone's circulation) and said, "I cannot do this!" I understood her anxiety. But the truth is, at 35,000 feet, I couldn't come up with another option. Some things we go *through* simply because there is no way go around them. "Through" is a terribly important word. No tragedy is forever. It may not be pleasant or desired, and there are after-effects that can be painful. But these words attributed to King David are crucial: "Yea, though I walk *through* the valley of the shadow of death, I will fear no evil . . . ." Sooner or later we do get through. No matter how desperate the storm on the Sea of Galilee seemed, the disciples survived. And this week, so did we.

Valuable lessons will be learned from this experience. In one of his press conferences, Governor Cuomo (of New York) said, "It seems like now we have the storm of the century every two years!" Then he added, "But, as the global climate changes, we will learn to change with it so as to be prepared and protected." He was saying that we will learn lessons from this experience. In fact, we already have.

For example, despite the fact that we are a coastal city, flooding has never been a huge issue here. So, up till now, backup generators have always been placed in basements. However, now that we know that floods are and will be an issue, builders and engineers will put backup generators above flood levels so that hospitals will not have to evacuate again. We will learn from this. Architects and builders will learn. Transportation and communication personnel will learn. The public will learn that when government officials say we need to evacuate, they know what they're talking about. Thus, lives will be saved next time around.

One of the valuable lessons we learned is something we already knew, but the storm reminded us. Governor Christie (of New Jersey) said it in a news conference: "There is a time for sorrow, and that time is now. But that time is not forever. Our sorrow will not displace our resilience!" You folks are made of tough stuff. Bruised? Yes. Battered? To be sure. But when the waters receded, you were still standing. "Our sorrow will not displace our resilience!" Valuable lessons have been and will be learned from this experience.

Nature's worst has revealed humanity's best. It always does. In our years together, I have witnessed you stand up and step forward in generous and loving ways for the people of Haiti, the people of Japan, the people of Prattsville, New York, the hungry children in Somalia, and the list goes on and on. Today in a special offering, you will do so again for our neighbors in the tri-state area. But isn't it inspiring to realize that just as you have stood up and stepped forward for others, today others all across the country are standing up and stepping forward for us?

Our mayor and our governor told stories of the bravery of first responders who walked into the teeth of the storm to rescue people, risking their lives for others whose lives were at risk. Offers have come in from all over the nation (as far away as Texas and California) from power companies, ambulance providers, Red Cross volunteers. Federal and local elected officials have stepped up to the plate, putting partisan politics behind them and joining hearts and hands to help people. The general secretary of our denomination sent out an e-mail to church members from coast to coast while the winds were raging and the waves were rising, asking people to pray for us *and* promising that Church World Service would be there to help those who suffered losses. Nature at its worst has revealed humanity at its best.

During the height of the storm, Page said to me, "Do you hear someone yelling?" I answered, "No. All I hear is the wind howling." She said, "I hear someone calling for help." We went to the sliding glass doors on our balcony. We overlook FDR Drive, which by then had become part of the East River. From there we saw a taxi stranded in rising waters that were already almost at the car's window level. The driver was yelling for help. It was a critical moment. The waves were whipping around his car. Page began to whistle at him, letting him know that someone saw him. I was feverishly dialing 911. But suddenly she said, "Wait! Look at that." We saw a man appear out of nowhere, almost like an angel, wading through those angry waters, two steps forward, one step back. He was calling out to the driver, "Hold on! Hold on!" Laboriously he made his way to the car, one stranger risking his life for another. He wrapped his arm around the driver's shoulder and slowly, carefully, walked him back to safety.

Some of you stayed here in Bay Hall to welcome people from our neighborhood. You served them coffee, showed them to the restrooms, helped them power up their cell phones and their laptops and their souls! Many of them said, "It means so much to be in a place where there is light, where there are people, and where we feel safe." It was the church being the church.

One of our members was without power for days. As the food in his freezer thawed, he used his gas stove to cook it and then distributed it to the elderly or vulnerable in his apartment building.

I personally have received e-mails and phone calls this week from people all across America. Some I have known for years. Others I have never heard of. But all contacted me to say, "We know what your people are going through. How can we help? What do you need? What can we do?"

One of the silver linings of a tragedy like this is that it restores our faith in people. Nature at its worst revealed humanity at its best.

Someone was in the storm with us. I quoted part of a text from the 23rd Psalm earlier. But let me quote the whole text: "Yea, though I walk through the valley of the shadow of death, I will fear no evil, for thou art with me!" That's how we get through life's valleys—because Someone who loves us is with us. And that's how we survive life's storms—because Someone bigger than the winds and the waves is in boat beside us. Mark said, "A furious storm arose, and the waves broke over the boat, so that it was nearly swamped. Jesus was in the stern, asleep. . . . The disciples woke him and said, 'Teacher, do you not care if we perish?' And he got up and rebuked the wind and said, 'Peace! Be still!' . . . And he said to his disciples, 'Why are you so afraid when I am in the boat with you?'"

It's an interesting scene. I've always wondered whether, when Jesus said, "Peace, be still," he was talking only to the winds and the waves or perhaps every bit as much to the disciples. They were fishermen, for the most part. They understood that violent storms descended quickly on the Sea of Galilee and left just as quickly. Storms come. It's the way life is. But storms do not last forever. Is it possible that Jesus was speaking primarily to the disciples? "Hang in there. This storm will end. But, while the winds rage and the waters rise, I am here with you. And as long as I am with you, you can live through any storm." That's our message. In this life, storms come. Winds rage. Waters rise. But we face it and survive it because Someone who loves us, who is bigger than anything life throws our way, is always in the boat with us.

On All Saints Sunday, it is our tradition to read the names of our church members who transitioned in the past year from this world to God's World. You heard those names read earlier, names of good people. Lovely people. Irreplaceable people. Each name left behind loved ones whose worlds are not the same now. They are struggling through the deep waters of loss and grief. What is God's word to those who mourn?

Over in Hoboken, New Jersey, which is still so ravaged by the hurricane, an aging woman was interviewed this week. She is at a temporary shelter. The reporter asked if she had any news about her home. The woman replied, "No. It may be gone. I don't know. But everything will be fine." The reporter then complimented her spirit of calm and courage, and the woman answered, "Many years ago, my son was killed in the war. A few months later, my husband died. That's when I discovered that when they went to be with God, God came to be with me. God got me through that, and God will get me through this. Everything will be fine." It was one of the most inspiring sermons I have ever heard. "When they went to be with God, God came to be with me." She found that when the winds rage and the waters rise, Someone is in boat with us, and that is our salvation. That is the healing news, the good news, on All Saints Sunday. "Yea, though I walk through the valley of the shadow of death, I will fear no evil, for thou art with me!"

We've been through a tough week, and there is still so much to do. We are a bit the worse for wear. We have suffered losses, some severe, but even in midst of it there are some things we can affirm:

• We survived.
• We will learn valuable lessons from this experience.
• Nature's worst revealed humanity's best.
• Whatever storms may come our way, Christ is always in the boat with us.

And his voice speaks to us with comfort, even as it did to the disciples long ago: "I'm here. I'm beside you. Peace, be still. It's going to be okay."

Reflection

1. What lessons do we learn through suffering that perhaps can be learned in no other way?

_____

_____

_____

_____

2. How can we best assist others who suffer (noting that human suffering takes a variety of forms)?

_____

_____

_____

_____

3. Name one promise in Scripture that you find most comforting in times of duress.

_____

_____

_____

_____

Attitudes

There are extremes of perspective that lie beyond the boundaries of realism. A negative or fatalistic worldview says that life is what it is, and my only happiness is accepting it as such. Recently I saw this saying on a T-shirt: "No one cares. They're just pretending." That is taking a negative outlook to an irrational extreme. The same happens on the other end of the spectrum. Pollyanna lives in some of the motivational chirpiness that we read in a variety of venues (usually named something like Thoughts for the Day): "You are confined only by the walls you build." "Every day in every way, the world is getting better and better." Statements like those take the positive characteristic of self-confidence to an irrational extreme.

Yes, life is what it is, but yes, I also have (or know where to find) the power to make my life different and better than it currently is. That is a middle ground rooted in faith. All is not perfect, nor is all corrupt. This place we inhabit is neither heaven nor hell, and we have options to lead our lives (and the lives of others) in either of those directions.

What I think about life does, to a great extent, determine what my experience of life will be like. What I look for is often what I will find. As the author of Proverbs reminds us, "What people think in their hearts, so they are" (23:7, see KJV). If I focus on love, simple logic suggests I will become more loving. By the same logic, if I focus on anger, I will become more antagonistic. My mental approach to tasks and opportunities (and whether or not I define issues I face as "tasks" or "opportunities") will set in motion inner energies that, though not necessarily determining, will contribute to success or defeat.

Obviously, of course, faith is a key component in the construction of attitude. The primary question for those with positive worldviews is not always "What can I do if I set my mind to it?" but rather "What do I believe God can do for, in, or through me?" Thus, a sense of confidence that builds a more hopeful and productive future is ultimately confidence in God.

Proceeding from that understanding, consider some biblical texts that help us explore where faith and personal attitude converge.

You Can Do All Things

I rejoice in the Lord greatly that now at length you have revived your concern for me; you were indeed concerned for me, but you had no opportunity. Not that I complain of want; for I have learned, in whatever state I am, to be content. I know how to be abased, and I know how to abound; in any and all circumstances I have learned the secret of facing plenty and hunger, abundance and want. I can do all things in him who strengthens me. (Philippians 4:10-13)

A defense attorney phoned his client, saying, "I have some good news and some bad news. Which do you want first?" The client said, "Give me the bad news first." His attorney answered, "Okay. The blood tests are back, and the blood at the scene of the crime matches your DNA." The client gasped and said, "What could possibly be good news after that?" The attorney replied, "Your cholesterol is down to 140."

There are times when a person is hard-pressed to find any good news in a situation. That must have been how Paul felt, writing from a prison cell, sentenced to die, loving and missing his people in Philippi, and knowing the hard times they would soon face. And yet, Paul challenged them to maintain a positive attitude even in the face of less than positive circumstances. In this passage, Paul builds on that message by suggesting how they might accomplish such. He says to them, "I rejoice greatly in the Lord, for I have learned to be content in all circumstances . . . . I can do all things through Christ, who strengthens me."

In all honesty, it is not easy to imagine saying that if you were in Paul's situation, or taking it seriously if you were in the situation of the Philippian Christians. Were we to confuse the word "content" with "happy," then probably no one would or even could make Paul's statement.

How can you be happy with the economy still in recovery mode and the job market still less than favorable for young people graduating from college or people over sixty who seek employment?

How can you be happy when a national terrorism alert is not infrequently at orange level?

How can you be happy when you read the news about Israel and Palestine, Syria, India and Pakistan, North Korea, Russia and Ukraine, Ethiopia and Darfur?

How can you be happy if you are a teenager being harassed or persecuted by other teenagers or teachers or pastors or parents because of your sexual orientation or gender identity?

How can you be happy if you are one of the almost one hundred million American adults battling depression?

How can you be happy if you are one of the forty-one million people suffering from HIV/AIDS?

How can you be happy with news reports every day of car bombings and kidnappings and random murders in the Mideast or school shootings in the United States?

Fill in your own blank of personal heartache or sorrow. Whatever cross you happen to be carrying, it is not always possible to be happy "in all circumstances."

However, Paul said it is possible to be "content." The Greek word he employed in this passage literally meant "at peace." Paul was not happy about his imprisonment, about the painful plights of his friends in Philippi, or about the coming persecution he knew they would have to suffer, but he was "at peace" because he knew the hands that held both him and them.

Many intriguing and inspiring stories are told in the aftermath of natural disasters. Similar scenes occurred following Hurricanes Katrina, Irene, Sandy, and other recent catastrophic events. Families are displaced. Many live in shelters such as public school gymnasiums, receiving minimal assistance (a place to sleep and some meals to eat until the waters recede and it is determined if they still have a house to go home to). But, invariably, volunteers on location in those temporary shelters tell of witnessing precisely the same thing. They see a family awaiting some news on the extent of the damage to their home. For all that family knows, their residence was one of the many completely destroyed. All that they possess may have been eradicated in a single hour of devastating weather. But there they are on cots in a gym. The mother holds their sleeping three-year-son on her shoulder, and the father reads to their five-year-old daughter who sits on his lap. One child sleeps peacefully while the other giggles at the story. How can they find such calm in the face of such calamity? What the volunteers describe is a picture with theological power. The children are probably not existentially "happy" in those treacherous circumstances, but they are "at peace" because they know the hands that hold them.

No matter what life threw his way, said Paul, "I have learned to be content in all circumstances." Not "happy" but "at peace." He knew (whether full or hungry, rich or poor, applauded or persecuted, in freedom or in a Roman prison cell) that God's hands held him tightly. So Paul was at peace. Thus he told the Philippians to surrender themselves (their lives, their fears, their dreams) to those same loving hands.

This is what separates Paul from your garden-variety motivational speaker who encourages people to pull themselves up by their own boot-straps. Paul, while not discouraging an appropriate sense of self-confidence, never recommends an exaggerated concept of our own inherent powers. In Paul's writings, we never find "I can if I think I can" philosophies of life; instead, we find a spirit of confidence in the limitless power of Christ. Paul says to the Philippians, "I can do all things *through Christ* who strengthens me."

One wonders if the Philippians were convinced. For that matter, are we? "I can do all things"? However hard I try, and however deep my faith may be, the truth is that I cannot do all things. I cannot leap tall buildings in a single bound. I cannot sing like Andrea Bocelli. I cannot paint like Chantal Joffe. I cannot hit a tennis ball like Serena Williams. I cannot write a check like Bill Gates. (Actually, I could write one; it's just that you couldn't use it for anything.) I can read through a copy of *Gray's Anatomy* and still not be able to perform surgery. I can watch all the instructional tapes in the world and still not hit a golf ball like Tiger Woods or Michelle Wie. I cannot make all people like me or even like one another. It really does not matter how deep my faith may be; there are things I simply cannot do. But is it possible that this is not what Paul actually intended to say? Instead, perhaps he was simply saying, "I can do what I have to do. I can do what I am called to do. I can do what I have been equipped to do. I can do what lies in front of me and cannot be avoided, however overwhelming or frightening. I can do more than I thought I could do if Jesus gives me the strength."

A familiar story tells of a family landscaping their lawn. They were working on a flower garden in front of the house. The garden was to be surrounded by large stones (not boulders, not unmanageable things, but certainly large enough to give you a good-sized backache if you aren't careful). The five-year-old son in the family watched as his daddy rolled those rocks, one by one, into place around the garden. Finally, he said, "Daddy, can I do it? Can I roll one of the rocks?"

With a slight and loving grin, his father said, "Here, son, you can try this one." Before the little boy started trying to push the rock, his dad offered another piece of advice. "I'm sure you can do it if you use all the strength at your disposal."

The little boy started. He had seen his father do it, and he was sure he could do it, too. But the rock was large and heavy, the ground was damp, and the stone would not budge however hard he huffed, puffed, and pushed. Finally, almost worn out, the little boy said, "You were wrong, Daddy. I can't move it."

His dad answered, "No, son. You didn't do what I told you. You didn't use all the strength at your disposal."

The child said, "What do you mean?" and his father answered, "You didn't ask me to help."

Sooner or later, we all have heavy rocks to move in our lives (at work, at home, in school, in the neighborhood, in the extended family, in church), and, on our own, we cannot budge them. But we can face whatever life throws our way if we use *all* the strength at our disposal, which means asking for the help of a heavenly Parent. Whatever you are facing in life, a Parent stands nearby waiting to lend a hand to help you face it, to help you do whatever has to be done. On our own, the tasks and challenges of life are sometimes overwhelming. But, as people of faith, we are not "on our own." The late Bishop C. E. Linney of the A.M.E. Church used to say, "The task before us is never as great as the Power behind us." Or, as Paul put it (enduring life in a prison cell), "I can do all things through Christ who strengthens me." So can we.

Reflection

1. What three things do you like best about yourself? How can each of those attributes be a tool for Christian discipleship?

_____

_____

_____

_____

2. Consider or discuss the meaning of "self-fulfilling prophecies." How do they contribute to/detract from a sense of satisfaction or wholeness in life?

_____

_____

_____

_____

3. Identify your primary source of strength in life. Defend your answer.

_____

_____

_____

_____

Beyond Asking Why

For everything there is a season, and a time for every matter under heaven:
a time to be born, and a time to die;
a time to plant, and a time to pluck up what is planted;
a time to kill, and a time to heal;
a time to break down, and a time to build up;
a time to weep, and a time to laugh;
a time to mourn, and a time to dance;
a time to cast away stones, and a time to gather stones together;
a time to embrace, and a time to refrain from embracing;
a time to seek, and a time to lose;
a time to keep, and a time to cast away;
a time to rend, and a time to sew;
a time to keep silence, and a time to speak;
a time to love, and a time to hate;
a time for war, and a time for peace. (Ecclesiastes 3:1-8)

Early in his junior year at college, my older son Adam was walking across campus at the University of North Carolina-Asheville with his friends Karen, Stephen, and Russell. They were on their way back to the dorm to watch some TV and get ready for Tuesday morning classes. As they walked on that cool, starlit mountain evening, they talked and laughed. My son said, "We were having a great time." Russell, one of the friends walking with him, was just a freshman. It was his first year at the university. One can imagine how excited he was as he adjusted to campus life. On his own for the first time. Growing up. Wondering about his major and meeting the right girl and planning his future. As the four of them walked toward the dorm, suddenly without warning Russell fell to his knees and then on his face. He was unconscious when he hit the ground. By the time the ambulance arrived, he had quit breathing. Adam saw them put his friend in the back of the rescue vehicle. He saw them as they used paddles on him. Off the ambulance raced, with friends left behind to worry and pray. A little while later, Adam heard that Russell (just a kid, only eighteen) had died.

To those who are in high school or beginning college, I apologize for what I'm about to write. But to those of us who are parents, a college freshman is still a child. It hasn't been that long since you held our hands when you crossed the street or since we changed your diapers or rocked you to sleep in our arms. Eighteen is young—awfully young. It sounds younger every day. At eighteen you are just getting started. You're standing in the narthex of life. You haven't even gotten into the main auditorium yet. Laughing, talking, and walking in the moonlight with friends, at eighteen a person is much, much too young to drop to the ground and die.

The story, sadly, is not that uncommon. It was only a few years ago that a beloved comedian, John Ritter, died. He was only fifty-four years old. That, too, is young. He had not even been sick. Ritter burst onto the scene in the hit TV show *Three's Company*. Afterward, there were some movies. After that came the loss of a marriage and something of a dry spell in his career. But suddenly he was again happily married, a loving father, and the star of a hit sitcom on ABC. John Ritter had experienced his own sort of resurrection, the beginning of a brand new life. Then, on a Thursday night, while filming his show, he simply fell over. His aorta came apart, the doctors said. Emergency measures quickly taken were not enough to save him. His life had come back together just in time for it to end. Where is the fairness in that?

Where's the fairness in the deaths of children at Sandy Hook Elementary in Newtown, Connecticut, who had gone to school where they should have been safe? But a very disturbed young man with access to a gun entered the school and randomly began to shoot.

Where's the fairness in a Colorado theater or on the campus of Virginia Tech University or in schools in California, Colorado, Maryland, or Washington state or in a Sikh temple in Wisconsin or in the countless acts of senseless violence we read about in every morning's paper or see on every evening's network news?

In all those stories and countless others like them, the friends and loved ones of innocent victims ask, "Why?" And that is, of course, an understandable question.

Who does not ask "Why?" when reading accounts of natural disasters or the latest terrorist activity of Al Qaeda or ISIS, when a local business operated by decent, caring people closes its doors because it can no longer compete with the mega chain store that opened a block away, or when a loved one receives a medical diagnosis for which there is no hope of a cure?

Recently, two stories in the local news appeared on the same morning. One was about the deaths of three young sisters in a limousine on their way back from a concert, hit by a drunken driver. The other was about a young high school football player who was accidentally shot by his best friend while on a hunting trip. In each story, heartbroken, weeping family and friends asked, "Why?"

Sometimes life does not seem fair. And however much you ponder or pray about it, it is still troubling. That's what made Rabbi Harold Kushner's book so popular a few years ago. It was called *When Bad Things Happen to Good People.* He wrote it following the death of his teenaged son, who lost his life to a rare illness called *progeria*, also known as "rapid aging." His little boy literally died of old age in front of Kushner's eyes, and there was not a thing he could do to stop it. As a person of faith, he could not understand why that tragedy would occur. And so he asked the question anyone would ask: "Why?" Why do such horrible things happen to people who do their best and live their best and love their best and do not deserve such pain?[6] The book quickly became a bestseller, which indicated that millions of others ask the same question.

It is not a new question. As far back as Job, religious thinkers have been asking why a good God would allow horrible things to transpire. The traditional responses are familiar, if not always altogether satisfying:

• Orthodoxy says you cannot know pleasure without the option for pain; otherwise, we are mere puppets in God's playhouse.
• Hebrew Scripture in the pre-Job era taught that suffering is a punishment for sin (which, in fact, some people still preach).
• The Deists (including the founding fathers of our country, people like Washington and Jefferson and Franklin) believed that God made us, but after that we're on our own, so good luck!
• Calvinists thought that some people are simply predestined to suffer.
• Christian Scientists taught that evil does not actually exist, so suffering is just an illusion.

There are all sorts of projected answers to the question that Job and others like Rabbi Kushner have asked: Why do bad things happen to good people?

Scholars call the author of Ecclesiastes "Koheleth" (which is a Hebrew word that simply means "the preacher"). Koheleth was a very different guy from Job. He did not ask "Why?" Instead, he looked at life from a realist's viewpoint. He said that bad things simply happen. So do good things. It's the way the world is made. It may not be the way we would like it, but it's the way it is.

"A time to be born, and a time to die; a time to plant, and a time to pluck up what is planted; a time to kill, and a time to heal; a time to break down, and a time to build up . . . ." There is a natural rhythm to his words, like breathing in and breathing out. Birth and death, sowing and reaping, weeping and laughing, war and peace. Koheleth said that's the way the world is made. Good and bad exist alongside each other. Mountains and valleys. Sunrise and sunset. It may not be the way we would like it, but it's the way it is. As I sometimes tell people, "This is not heaven yet."

Obviously none of us desires hardship or suffering. Three members of a local church were chatting one day at the barbershop. One of them said, "When you die and your friends view you in the casket, what do you want them to say?" Robert answered, "I want them to say, Robert was a good church worker, a good husband, and a good family man." Frank said, "I want them to say, Frank was a wonderful teacher, had a great sense of humor, and made a difference in the church and the community." Finally, Tom said, "I want them to say, Look! He's moving!" (Tom's response is similar to Woody Allen's line: "I'm not afraid of dying; I just don't want to be there when it happens.")

Most of us are like Tom, and understandably so. We do not want suffering to come. But the truth is, want it or not, it still comes. And, like Job, we wonder why.

To be perfectly honest, though, even if we could answer the question "Why," what difference would it make? It would not in any sense take away the sadness or the pain that we might feel. It would not in any way change the outcome of things.

A lovely young woman was murdered during her senior year at a major national university. I was her parents' minister. The girl's mother was not concerned about securing justice by having the murderer (her daughter's roommate) put to death. She even pleaded with the court not to impose capital punishment. I remember what that mother said to me about her decision to request leniency: "The courts will do what the courts will do, but in the end I will not have my daughter returned to me." She had moved beyond the question "Why?"

That is how Koheleth dealt with the question of evil and suffering, not by asking "Why?" but rather by asking "What now?" Evil simply happens in this world. Jesus himself said so: "The poor will be with you always" (Matt 26:11). "There will be wars and rumors of wars" (Matt 24:6). So the issue is not so much learning why those things happen but rather learning how to cope when they do, what to take from moments of defeat that will help us achieve future victories, how to use our suffering as equipment to live more effectively and to heal others who suffer, too.

If one were to request a show of hands in most congregations, what percentage might go up if the minister asked these questions:

Who here has ever lost a parent? A spouse? A child? A job? A marriage? Some measure of your physical health?

Who here has ever taken medications for depression? Had serious surgery? Almost lost your life in an accident? Fought in a war?

Readers who answered "Yes" to one or more of those questions are not alone. Almost every adult inside or outside a church would answer affirmatively to at least one of those questions. No matter how bad life may seem at the moment, we're not the only person who ever carried a similar cross. We're not the only person who ever suffered. And if we knew "why" any of those tragedies in one's life occurred, would it change even to a single iota the fact that the tragedies did occur? The point is this: What have we done with our tragedies, or what have we allowed them to do to us?

Someone told me a story some time ago that I have not been able to verify. Perhaps some of you will recognize the name. My friend told me of a man named Chester Mayfield who, he said, was a minor league baseball player in the mid-1950s. As my friend told the story, Mr. Mayfield was a shoo-in to have a spectacular future in the Major Leagues. Apparently he could hit like Mickey Mantle and run the bases like Jackie Robinson. But, just before he was to be called up to the big leagues, he was involved in a hunting accident and lost his left arm. With that, he lost his dreams of being a major leaguer. Many of us (perhaps most of us) would have lost all hope under similar circumstances. According to the man telling the story, though, Chester Mayfield went on to spend his whole life joyfully, productively working with handicapped children and making their lives bright. Whenever anyone asked how he managed to deal with his personal tragedy, he would answer, "God gave me the strength to survive, and then God asked me to pass that strength along to these children."

Why did Chester Mayfield have to lose his arm? Who knows? My answer would be that it was simply the kind of tragic accident that too often happens in this world. It was not planned or willed by a Higher Power. Sometimes bad things happen to people. But if we did know why the accident occurred, would that knowledge have made his arm grow back in place? The point is that even in his tragedy, Chester found two things: the loving, healing presence of God *and* the wisdom to use his suffering as a tool to help other people who suffer.

"To everything there is a season," wrote the author of Ecclesiastes, "and a time for every purpose under heaven. A time to be born, and a time to die . . . a time to weep, and a time to laugh; a time to mourn, and a time to dance . . . a time of war, and a time of peace."

Good happens. And evil happens as well. It's simply how life works. When pain and suffering arrive, we can surrender to sadness. Lots of people who exist as emotional zombies have done just that. But we also have the option to lean on a Power beyond our own and learn the lessons only suffering can teach. A proverb says, "Suffering either makes us bitter, or it makes us better." A Minor League baseball player on his way up who lost his arm in a tragic accident chose the latter way of looking at life, and thus years later he was able to say, "God gave me the strength to survive, and then God asked me to pass that strength along."

Reflection

1. Reflect on an event of significant human suffering and/or a personal experience of suffering or loss. How did you feel when you experienced or read about it? What questions sprang to mind? What actions did you take?

_____

_____

_____

_____

2. As you reflect on that event, is your understanding of God troubling or comforting?

_____

_____

_____

_____

3. Reflect on the personal and theological meanings expressed in this poem:

> I walked a mile with Pleasure.
> She chatted all the way,
> But left me none the wiser
> For all she had to say.
>
> I walked a mile with Sorrow,
> And ne'er a word said she,
> But oh! The things I learned from her,
> When Sorrow walked with me.[7]

_____

_____

_____

_____

Seeing People, Learning Lessons

Let brotherly love continue. Do not neglect to show hospitality to strangers, for thereby some have entertained angels unawares. Remember those who are in prison, as though in prison with them; and those who are ill treated, since you also are in the body. (Hebrews 13:1-3)

In a city like the one where I live, most growth is up. So all of us spend a lot of time on elevators. Thus we all know elevator etiquette: Do not speak to anyone. Do not make eye contact. Stare at the numbers as the floors change.

I read a list recently of alternative elevator strategies. It was titled "Suggested Things to Do Next Time You Are on a Crowded Elevator." Let me share a few of those intriguing suggestions with you:

• Keep whistling the first verse of "It's a Small World."
• Crack open your briefcase or purse, peek inside, and ask, "Oh my gosh, what happened to my snake?"
• Greet everyone on the elevator with a smile and warm handshake, and ask them to call you "Admiral."
• Loudly say the word "Ding" at each floor.
• Say to the person standing next to you, "These things always give me motion sickness."

If you decide to try any of those, let me know how it turns out.

Most of us have elevator stories. In a city of eight million people, it's possible to bump into a long-lost friend on a random elevator. One of our staff members not long ago got stuck on an elevator for over an hour and a half. Most of us have gotten off on the wrong floor, or pushed UP when we meant to push DOWN. Let me share with you three of my own elevator experiences, three random encounters that caused me to think about life and loneliness and fear and fellowship and faith. In each of those encounters and in truly seeing people as they were, I learned valuable lessons about life.

The lesson from Hebrews (about "entertaining angels unaware") comes to mind because I think I occasionally bump into angels on elevators. Not the kind you usually think about—guardian angels with wings and harps and halos. If I ever reported seeing one of those on an elevator, one of my church members would doubtless suggest that I take the express elevator right to the Blanton-Peale Center (the Counseling Center associated with our church). But wings and harps and halos are not essentially how the Bible describes angels. Oh sure, the choir that sang over Bethlehem on the first Christmas may have looked that way, but even the Easter angels at the empty tomb were simply described as "two men in white." And almost every time angels showed up in stories from Hebrew Scripture, they were mistaken merely as strangers in town. Throughout most of both the Old Testament and the New, the word "angel" simply means "God's messenger." No wings. No halos. Sometimes they are not even all that holy. It reminds me of Lucy in the *Peanuts* cartoon, who yells at Charlie Brown, "I am, too, an angel. And if you don't say so, I'll punch your nose, you blockhead!" Though that way of relating is not seen as exactly angelic in nature, Lucy was still a bearer of truth.

So, with that understanding in mind (that sometimes angels are merely real-life human beings who convey Truth from God), it becomes a bit easier to understand the words of the author of Hebrews when he refers to encountering "angels unaware," angels that didn't look like angels, whom we would not have assumed to be angels, but who got a message through from God to us.

Stepping onto the elevator outside Bay Hall (a fellowship area in our church building), I encountered a young woman already on board who stood silently staring at her cell phone. "Which floor?" I asked her as I prepared to push the buttons. She answered, "I don't know. It doesn't matter." It seemed an odd response. But I simply pushed the button for my floor, then (as cheerfully as I knew how) said to her, "Well, then, you get to go to floor 10." She shot me a glance that seemed more frightened than anything else and said quickly and curtly, "Why are you talking to me? Leave me alone!" I did as she requested until the doors opened on the tenth floor. Stepping off, I turned around, looked at her, and said, "I'm a minister here. We exist to help people who need our help. So if there's ever anything we can do for you, just get on this elevator, push almost any button at all, and someone will be waiting who wants to help you." She looked back at me. Her expression softened. She opened her mouth as if she were starting to speak, but then she didn't. Her eyes simply returned to her phone, and the doors closed. My guess is she was trying to find the Blanton-Peale Center and was probably looking up their floor number on her cell phone. She did not know me and felt awkward about telling me where she was going. I get that. But what I remember is her response that looked and sounded like fear. And I remember wondering as I walked away, "Who did I remind her of? Who in her past made her so frightened?" Was there some person in her long-ago history, maybe a man, who had abused her in some way? And alone in an elevator with a man she did not know, had those memories and fears come rushing back?

My encounter with her reminded me of the wounds and scars that can be inflicted on people when they're young. Sometimes those wounds and scars last a lifetime and affect, even impair, every relationship that comes afterward. One out of every three preteen girls in our country and one out of every five preteen boys are physically or sexually abused. The statistics of psychological abuse are dramatically higher. And abuse can cause everything from paranoia to promiscuity, from drug abuse to self-abuse, from academic failure to emotional depression. The author of Hebrews encouraged his readers, "Continue to remember . . . those who are mistreated as if you yourselves were suffering." Encountering that young woman on the elevator challenged me never to forget "those who are mistreated," especially innocent and vulnerable children, because what is done to them can create a cycle of pain that lasts throughout the years. And so we are called, I think, to advocate for them, to stand up, to speak out, to intervene, to love. "Keep on loving one another," the biblical writer said, "for by doing so some people have entertained angels."

The second elevator encounter was with an older woman. She pushed the button for the fifth floor. I then pushed the button for my office on the tenth. She looked at me and said, "You're going all the way to the top. I'm just going halfway there." Then, on the elevator with a stranger, she literally broke into song: "Up is up and down is down, and halfway's neither up nor down." Not having the slightest idea how to respond to that, I simply answered, "What a fun little tune." She said, "My parents taught it to me when I was a child. I will never forget that. They were good people. They always paid a lot of attention to me." The doors opened. As she stepped off, she looked back and said, "Thank you for noticing that I was here."

She was lonely and felt unnoticed. And she thanked me for not merely staring at the numbers as they changed and, thus, shutting her out. She thanked me for simply paying a brief moment's attention to her, for hearing her song, and for listening to her story about years long ago and people loved and lost.

In our land where 75 percent of adults claim to feel somewhat disconnected, unnoticed and lonely, she reminded me that it never requires too much of us just to notice people, to smile, to say "Good morning," or simply to acknowledge that they exist and that someone cares. That's an important truth to remember. Maybe she was an "angel unaware."

On Sunday mornings when I go down from my office on the tenth floor to the hallway that leads to the sanctuary, the elevator inevitably stops and the door opens on the sixth floor where our children's classes are. Parents and their kids will crowd into the elevator on their way to worship. We back one another into the corners like sardines in a can, always laughing, and always saying how it would be physically impossible to fit one more in. One Sunday morning recently, a little girl said to her mom, "Wow, this place is so crowded!" Her mother answered: "I know. Isn't it great to be surrounded by these people?"

That mother understood the meaning of *community*, which is at the heart of what it means to be a church, a place where we can bring all our fears or all our loneliness and be surrounded by the healing presence, grace, love, and support of people. In this sacred fellowship, the fears are less overwhelming and the loneliness vanishes away.

In my life, in my times of crisis, I have found three human factors I can lean on. Obviously, of course, I lean on my faith, on prayer, and on confidence in the healing nearness of God. But, as Barbara Streisand sang, "people need people," and in times of personal crisis I have found strength to survive from three human sources: family, one or two very close and trusted friends, and church (this community of people who are on the same journey, who love without judging, and who help without stopping to count the cost). "Isn't it great to be surrounded by these people?"

A few years ago, following a service in which we installed new members of the Marble Church Board, one of those newly installed individuals said to me, "When the hands of clergy and other board members were laid upon my shoulders, and when I heard the congregation vow to support me with their faith and prayers, I felt like I was surrounded by a company of angels." I think she was. We often are thus surrounded, both in sacred services at church and also in ordinary moments in the world. In classrooms and checkout lines, in subways and supermarkets, in hair salons and hospital waiting rooms, and even in elevators, God's Truth comes to us in surprising ways through unexpected people. It is incumbent upon us to develop a perceptive perspective, to see people as they actually are, and thus to learn the lessons that their lives can teach. Put another way, our challenge is simply not to miss the moments when God's messages come to us through "angels unaware."

Reflection

1. Identify a moment when you had an unexpected encounter that clarified your perspective or taught you a valuable lesson about one of life's issues.

_____

_____

_____

_____

2. Discuss or consider the reasons we might overlook or ignore another individual. What are some possible ramifications of doing this both in our own lives as well as in the lives of those who are overlooked?

_____

_____

_____

_____

3. What is the meaning of the phrase "the words behind the words"? How can we learn to hear what a person intends rather than merely what they say?

_____

_____

_____

_____

Thankfulness
(Everyday Blessings)

And he said to his disciples, "Therefore I tell you, do not be anxious about your life, what you shall eat, nor about your body, what you shall put on. For life is more than food, and the body more than clothing. Consider the ravens: they neither sow nor reap, they have neither store-house nor barn, and yet God feeds them. Of how much more value are you than the birds! And which of you by being anxious can add a cubit to his span of life? If then you are not able to do as small a thing as that, why are you anxious about the rest? Consider the lilies, how they grow; they neither toil nor spin; yet I tell you, even Solomon in all his glory was not arrayed like one of these. But if God so clothes the grass which is alive in the field today and tomorrow is thrown into the oven, how much more will he clothe you, O men of little faith! And do not seek what you are to eat and what you are to drink, nor be of anxious mind. For all the nations of the world seek these things; and your Father knows that you need them. Instead, seek his kingdom, and these things shall be yours as well. Fear not, little flock, for it is your Father's good pleasure to give you the kingdom." (Luke 12:22-32)

There once was a fellow named Fred
Who wore rubies all over his head.
His wife said, "Bizarre!
How inadequate you are!
You ought to wear diamonds instead!"

Houseboat
    Land yacht
        Palatial mansion

Infinite resources
"Show me the money"
"Supersize me"

The common vernacular of our culture indicates that in our minds, bigger is better and enough is rarely enough. And rather than being thankful for what we have, most of us are hopeful of having more. "You ought to wear diamonds instead!"

Jesus said just the opposite. He said pretty much what Rhoda Blecker wrote in an issue of *Guideposts Daily Devotionals*. She said, "My everyday blessings are blessings every day." That's what Jesus was getting at when he told people they were too concerned about the big banquet to come someday but were ignoring the food at their disposal every day: "Consider the birds of air. God feeds them every day. Are you not of more value than they?" Or they were concerned about what they would wear and how fancy it might appear: "And consider lilies of field. Even Solomon in all his glory was not as well dressed as one of these. . . . Fear not, little flock, for it is the Father's good pleasure to give you the kingdom." They focused on what they wanted (more and bigger and better), but failed to recognize what they needed ("It is the Father's good pleasure to give you the kingdom"). God was supplying their needs every day—food, clothing, a place to sleep, family, friends, life, and just waking up each morning to a new day with its unique potential and simple pleasures. In their desire for more, they overlooked their everyday blessings.

Some time ago I officiated at the memorial service of a wonderful woman in our congregation. Her name was Cynthia Antonio. Her daughter, Sheril, shared personal remarks about her mother with the congregation, in which she stated, "Mom always said, 'Thank God for this and that.'" What a beautiful and spiritual outlook on life. She was aware of and grateful for the little things, the too often overlooked things, the taken for granted things that make life rich and warm. "Thank God for this and that.'"

Admittedly, maintaining that sort of spirit is not always easy, especially in a world like ours. I heard someone say, "It's hard to remain thankful if you read the morning news." I get that. Economy and illness, prejudice and violence, political gridlock at home and political instability abroad, ISIS and Putin and Syria and Yemen and all the rest. But, while not living in denial as if those things are not real, one of the keys to surviving in a world like this is to realize that for all the bad we see around us all the time, there is also a lot of good and a lot of beauty. There are everyday blessings for those who, as Jesus put it, "have ears to hear and eyes to see." Case in point: before the 2014 ceasefire in the Holy Land, a Palestinian child was quoted in the news. She said, "It always makes me happy after the bombs stop to hear birds singing." What a little thing birdsong seems in the midst of the desperate circumstances of her world. But, after the bombs stopped, the music of birds reminded her that she had made it, she was still alive, and there was still reason for hope. "Consider birds of the air," said Jesus. Let's say it again: one of the keys to surviving in a world like this is to realize that for all the bad we see around us all the time, there are still everyday blessings for those who have "ears to hear and eyes to see."

If we have the perspective of Fred and his wife, that more is better and enough is never enough, then happiness, peace, and contentment will always remain just out of reach. Jesus was clear in saying that we will never experience the beauty of simply being alive until we are able to celebrate the beauty of everyday blessings—"the birds of the air, and the lilies of the fields," and music, laughter, rainbows, hugs, and the people who provide them.

A former church member of mine years ago was named Larry. Larry lived by himself in a tiny house on a beautiful acre of land. He always wore a light blue shirt and khaki pants. That was all he owned. I was never sure how many of those shirts and trousers he owned, but they were all he ever wore. Most of the time, he rode around town on a moped (though he did own, but rarely used, a '60s vintage VW Bug). Lots of folks found him eccentric, odd, or worse. I remember hearing someone say of him once, "He's like a five-story building with a three-story elevator." In truth, he was not like that at all. He was just a man with simple tastes, nothing extravagant, who saw blessings in little things that most of us tend to miss. His house was neat and clean, but maybe 500 square feet maximum. It was all he needed. He lived alone, and, like my own dad used to say, "You can't live in but one room at a time." He had a small house and a simple wardrobe, but his property was a showplace of flowers and shrubbery and summer vegetable gardens and blooming, exotic trees and birdbaths and birdhouses. Those were his priorities. He saw and celebrated the beauties and blessings of nature all around him.

"Consider the birds of the air and the lilies of the fields," said Jesus, and Larry understood exactly what Jesus was talking about. I remember standing beside him in his backyard once, surrounded by buds and blooms and blossoms everywhere I looked, and hearing him say, "These things make me rich." When Larry died, the very people who had questioned his values (and even his intelligence) during his life almost unanimously confessed that Larry may have been the wisest of us all.

Ours is not a perfect world, but it is a beautiful world. None of us live in perfect cities, but if it's "home," then to us it is a wonderful city. We do not attend perfect churches, but in most of our churches we still find people who are present for one another in times of need. We find community, a family of faith, listening ears, shoulders to lean on, and limitless love. Wouldn't it be tragic to be here on this journey and not see all those everyday blessings?

A friend of mine, a devoted Christian in most senses, is simply unsure about eternal life. Personally, I think that doctrine is one of the centerpieces of our faith and all the world's great faiths (Judaism, Islam, Hinduism, etc.). He, though, is unsure. And yet he is genuinely one of the happiest people I have ever known. We've known each other a long time, so we have had this conversation about the afterlife more than once. I ask how he can be so full of joy while thinking that this life may be all there is and one day it all might end. He always answers, "That's why I look for happiness every day of this life. What if this is my only chance for it—for drinking in beauty, for feeling love, for hearing music, and for knowing laughter? If this life is my one chance for happiness, I am determined not to miss out on it!"

As a believer in Jesus and the truth of his resurrection, I am convinced that this life is not all there is. Beyond this world is another World too beautiful even to conceive, let alone describe. And yet my friend's philosophy is not without merit. Life rushes by too quickly, and there is so much good in it. So, if we have the chance each new day to drink in beauty, to feel love, to hear music, to know laughter, or to embrace all the everyday blessings that are ours, then may God give us the wisdom not to miss out on it. "Consider the birds of the air and the lilies of the field," and all life's everyday blessings, Jesus said.

Reflection

1. What issues/forces impede a spirit of thankfulness?

_____

_____

_____

_____

2. Name three blessings that make your life better and brighter on a daily basis.

_____

_____

_____

_____

3. While neither ignoring life's pains nor denying its goodness, how can we create a personal focus that helps us survive the pains and enhance an awareness of goodness?

_____

_____

_____

_____

Grace

Finally, my brothers and sisters, rejoice in the Lord. To write the same things to you is not irksome to me, and is safe for you. Look out for the dogs, look out for the evil-workers, look out for those who mutilate the flesh. For we are the true circumcision, who worship God in spirit, and glory in Christ Jesus, and put no confidence in the flesh. Though I myself have reason for confidence in the flesh also. If any other man thinks he has reason for confidence in the flesh, I have more: circumcised on the eighth day, of the people of Israel, of the tribe of Benjamin, a Hebrew born of Hebrews; as to the law a Pharisee, as to zeal a persecutor of the church, as to righteousness under the law blameless. But whatever gain I had, I counted as loss for the sake of Christ. Indeed I count everything as loss because of the surpassing worth of knowing Christ Jesus my Lord. For his sake I have suffered the loss of all things, and count them as refuse, in order that I may gain Christ and be found in him, not having a righteousness of my own, based on law, but that which is through faith in Christ, the righteousness from God that depends on faith; that I may know him and the power of his resurrection, and may share his sufferings, becoming like him in his death, that if possible I may attain the resurrection from the dead. Not that I have already obtained this or am already perfect; but I press on to make it my own, because Christ Jesus has made me his own. Brothers and sisters, I do not consider that I have made it my own; but one thing I do, forgetting what lies behind and straining forward to what lies ahead, I press on toward the goal for the prize of the upward call of God in Christ Jesus. (Philippians 3:1-14)

Not long ago I was browsing through a catalogue from a Christian Speakers' Bureau in Nashville, Tennessee. As I turned page by page, I recognized most of the names of the speakers the group represents, from Margaret Bush to Jack Canfield to Joe Torre and on and on. I was, however, unfamiliar with one of their clients whose first name is Michael. His bio read that his father was a Mafia figure years ago in New York City. That is the environment in which Michael grew up. When he finished college, he went on to med school. But during that time, his father died. So, instead of finishing school and becoming a physician, Michael came back home to New York and assumed his dad's role as a leader in organized crime. Eventually he was arrested, convicted of various serious crimes, and sent to prison for seven years. There he was—still a young man, for most of his history involved with organized crime, his future still devoted to it, sitting behind bars at Attica. One night another inmate said to him, "You got big problems, brother. Why don't you turn them over to God?"

Michael laughed out loud at the idea and answered, "What have I ever done that would get God on my side?"

The older man replied, "That's the beauty of it. God is on your side before you do the first thing to get him there."

That inmate at Attica accurately described the wonder of Grace. *God is on your side before you do the first thing.* It was a turning point for Michael, who did not return to organized crime but instead travels all across America telling people about the unearned, transforming love of God who is on our side before we do the first thing.

Paul had done religious things before becoming a Christian. As he told the Philippians, he had been "ceremoniously marked on the eighth day, of the people of Israel, of the tribe of Benjamin, a Hebrew of Hebrews, a law-abiding Pharisee." But, despite outward appearances, Paul admitted that deep down in his heart other things resided: things like anger, jealousy, arrogance, prejudice, and hatred. As he confessed to his friends in Philippi, he was "a persecutor of Christians" and had, in fact, been an accomplice to the murder of St. Stephen. The truth is, there was so much darkness and despair in his soul that, in Paul's own words, he said he felt like "the chief of sinners." But then something happened. A Spirit larger than his own reached down on the road to Damascus, hugged Paul to himself, held him close, whispered to him of forgiveness, and turned all the shadows inside him into light. "All the rest I consider as rubbish," he wrote, but rejoiced instead (as he put it) that I do "not have a righteousness of my own . . . but that which is through faith in Christ!"

What did that mean? It meant that Paul finally figured out the idea behind a bumper sticker I saw: "God Loves Us Anyhow!" We don't have to be good enough, moral enough, smart enough, rich enough, successful enough, or anything enough. God's love comes to us not *because of* what we are, but *in spite of* it. Paul learned that Christ was on his side before he did the first thing.

Mildred, a second grade Sunday school teacher in Arizona, wrote in a devotional magazine about having her students do a month-long prayer journal—each of them writing down every single prayer that they prayed throughout the entire month. Once the journals were turned in, she read through them. In the journal of one little boy in her class she found this entry: "Dear God, please ignore my mom's prayers to make me a better boy. I'm sure You and I are pretty happy with me the way I am!" That child must have read Philippians. He understood that God loves us in spite of ourselves. God is on our side before we do the first thing. *Just as I am, Thou wilt receive.*

There's another thing Paul wanted his friends in Philippi to understand. As we have mentioned before, Paul (a prisoner) wrote to people who were by-and-large struggling, often frightened (and rightly so), and facing an organized Roman persecution of unprecedented proportion. He wrote as one who suffers to people who suffer. As such, he reminded them that *grace is the presence of Christ with us in life's tough times.* He said that we "share in the sufferings of Christ . . . so somehow to attain the resurrection of the dead." Jesus suffered like we do, insisted Paul, so he understands what we experience when we hurt. And since his sufferings wound up in victory (the victory of the resurrection), our sufferings can wind up in victory, too. Paul reminded the Philippians that grace is the presence of Christ with us in life's tough times.

Renewed interest emerged regarding the missing-person case of the young child Etan Patz who simply disappeared in our city decades ago. The renewed interest was the result of the trial of a man who has confessed to Etan's abduction and murder. How difficult it must have been on the parents shortly after their son disappeared. Each passing day made it less and less likely that he would ever be found. Those parents were proud of their child and loved him deeply and dearly. It is hard to imagine how devastated they must have been in the wake of his disappearance and likely death.

The whole nation joined our region not long ago in mourning the tragic, foolish, and unnecessary deaths of schoolchildren in Newtown, Connecticut. That was a quiet and traditionally safe community, the sort of place where parents feel confident rearing their children. How heartbroken we all were when we realized that the actions of one disturbed individual shattered the safety and confidence we all cherished.

How devastated the parents and loved ones of Kayla Mueller must be when remembering their lovely daughter, who sought only to advocate for and assist the vulnerable and abused in Syria and suffered death at the hands of ISIS because of her spirit of compassion. How crushed so many others must also be when photos or videos are released of journalists being beheaded by radical militants, or innocent people in Uganda being taken off the bus and murdered simply because of their faith, or innocent children in Pakistan being shot in their classrooms by terrorists, or journalists in Paris being viciously murdered by religious fanatics, or as many as two thousand innocents in Nigeria being massacred by murderers.

How tormented must be the loved ones of people who were traveling when their airplanes just suddenly disappeared from the radar screen?

And what of the people who in recent days have lost possessions and family members because of hurricanes, tornadoes, or tsunamis?

Is there a word of hope to be spoken to those who hurt and grieve? To be sure, there is no quick fix. But there is a word, and it is this: Jesus is with us in our suffering, and even in the face of death there is still victory. That is exactly the testimony Paul made to the Philippians. We "share in the sufferings of Christ . . . so somehow to attain the resurrection of the dead." In our pain, he is with us, and someday beyond the final pain we will be with him!

Having said a word about grace, Paul went on to say a word about a different but related topic. "Forgetting what is behind, and straining forward to what is ahead, I press on toward the goal for the upward prize in Christ Jesus." In Paul's understanding, *grace always precedes discipleship.*

One of the best people I know was for a while profane, violent, dishonest, and frequently in significant trouble with the police. Today, however, he is a leader in his community and his church, the sort of person in whose hands I would trust my life without a moment's hesitation. Some time ago, he and I talked about his dramatic turnaround. He credits it all to his wife. He said, "She loved me so much when I was bad that I started trying to be good, just for her."

Paul felt the same way about his life of discipleship. Christ loved him so much when he was bad that for the rest of his life he tried to be good, just for Jesus. "Forgetting what is behind, and straining forward to what is ahead, I press on toward the goal for the upward prize in Christ Jesus." We do not live Christian lives to earn God's love; instead, we are so overwhelmed by and thankful for God's love that we live Christian lives just for God. Grace comes first. Discipleship is always our response to it. As we read in 1 John, "We love God because God first loved us." And that love naturally translates into action. Loving that is not backed up by our lives is not loving at all.

Recently I was sent an Internet story attributed to Max Lucado. It revealed in narrative form what the New Testament means when it uses the word "grace." The story was of Maria and Christina, a mother and daughter from Brazil. Christina was a strong-willed young woman, and Maria was a devoted and deeply caring mother. When Christina was sixteen, she and her mom became involved in an argument after which the young girl walked out of their home, claiming she would live her own life and make her own rules. Maria knew that a teenaged girl with little education could easily and quickly sink to the bottom of life, just to survive. She could easily fall into the drug culture or into prostitution or both. So Maria set out in search of her daughter.

Before she began her journey, Maria took what little money she had to the photograph booth at a local store. She used all her money to make a stack of black and white pictures of herself. Then Maria began going from city to city in Brazil, entering all the bars and hotels and placing her picture in lobbies and women's restrooms.

Her suspicions about her daughter were accurate. Christina, with no money and no way to support herself, had fallen into prostitution in order to stay alive. One evening she descended a long flight of steps in a Brazilian hotel, and at the bottom of the staircase she saw a familiar face. Taped to a mirror next to the bar was a picture of her mother. Christina walked over to the mirror and removed the photograph. Turning it over, she read a hand-scribbled message from Maria. It simply said, "I don't care what you've done. Please come home." And with that, Christina used the money in her purse to buy a bus ticket home.

That is grace. God doesn't care what we've done or failed to do. God keeps the door open and the lights on, hoping that all the children stumbling their way through the darkness will come home.

That's what Paul told the Philippians. Grace, God's unconditional love for us, God's open heart and open arms, comes first. And once we finally realize how deeply we are loved, we begin the journey home. "Forgetting what is behind, and straining forward to what is ahead, I press on toward the goal for the upward prize in Christ Jesus."

Reflection

1. Explain your biblical/theological understanding of the word "grace."

_____

_____

_____

_____

2. Explain your biblical/theological understanding of the word "transformation." Identify a biblical character whose life was positively transformed. Defend your answer.

_____

_____

_____

_____

3. "Sanctification" is a theological term indicating "the spiritual journey toward perfection." How can you sense that principle being lived out in your life? How do Christian believers cope with/live within the limitations of our humanity?

_____

_____

_____

_____

Section Three

Divine Expectations

Isaiah writes about the moment when he heard the voice of God saying, "Whom shall I send, and who will go for me?" And Isaiah answered, "Here am I, LORD. Send me." It is an inspiring passage that has been the text of many a stirring sermon, not to mention one of the most motivating hymns since the days of the Wesleys:

> Here I am, Lord. Is it I, Lord?
> I have heard you calling in the night.
> I will go, Lord, if you send me.
> I will hold your people in my heart.[8]

What we sometimes fail to consider is the context in which Isaiah's text occurs. It begins with the words, "In the year that King Uzziah died," and continues to refer to the shaking of foundations, houses filled with smoke, institutional woe, ecclesiastical lost-ness, and personal and corporate guilt. In short, the calls that come from God are not always simple or ceremonial. Those calls challenge us to do difficult things often in challenging settings. If God only asked us to do what is easy, everyone would say "Yes."

And yet embedded within the call of God is a spirit of mercy (even affirmation). God assured Isaiah, "Your guilt is taken away, and your sin is forgiven." Furthermore, God told Isaiah that he was chosen to do a redeeming work among the people of Israel. That which God asks us to do will not always be easy (nor often desired), but it will always be sacred. Furthermore, it will endow us with a sense of purpose and meaning.

In this section, let's think together about Divine expectations and faithful responses.

Called by Mercy

*And you he made alive, when you were dead through the trespasses
and sins in which you once walked, following the course of this world,
following the prince of the power of the air, the spirit that is now at
work in the sons of disobedience. Among these we all once lived in the
passions of our flesh, following the desires of body and mind, and so we
were by nature children of wrath, like the rest of mankind. But God,
who is rich in mercy, out of the great love with which he loved us, even
when we were dead through our trespasses, made us alive together with
Christ (by grace you have been saved), and raised us up with him, and
made us sit with him in the heavenly places in Christ Jesus, that in
the coming ages he might show the immeasurable riches of his grace in
kindness toward us in Christ Jesus. For by grace you have been saved
through faith; and this is not your own doing, it is the gift of God—
not because of works, lest anyone should boast. (Ephesians 2:1-9)*

Kyrie Eleison ("Lord, have mercy!") is one of the historic prayers of the
church, often associated with the season of Lent, which can be a dark and
brooding time of the year. It is a season of penitence and prayer, a time for
fasting and facing up to our personal sins and shortcomings. But right in
the middle of Lent stands the cross, a symbol of the inexhaustible love of
Jesus Christ and the lengths to which that love would go to rescue us from
our guilt. So the primary theme of Lent, as well as of the whole Christian
year, is always *mercy*—how the reality of our failings comes face to face with
the reality of God's love.

Often when we hear the word "mercy" we think immediately of another
word, "forgiveness" (which a poet called "the scent of the violet on the heel
that crushed it"). The truth is, however, that whereas forgiveness is merciful,
mercy is more than mere forgiveness. It is instead "acceptance"—to accept,
affirm, and even love the other person, just as they are and sometimes in
spite of how they are.

An acquaintance in the ministry told me of a man who belonged to a
church he served many years ago. During that time, the man intentionally

hurt my friend. He told lies about the clergyman and sought to undermine his ministry at that church just because the two of them disagreed about some little issue in an obscure committee. For several years, the church member continually and consistently made life hellish for the pastor. Likewise, throughout his ministry at that church and for years afterward, my friend carried a burden of deep, dark resentment against the other man, a resentment that bordered on hatred. Years later, the two of them bumped into one another. Here's how the minister told the story:

"Something inside me told me the time had come. So I walked across the room and extended my hand to my old enemy, unsure of whether or not he would take it. Almost to my surprise, and certainly to my relief, he did. And for a long time that day we stood and talked and laughed and shared stories. Neither of us ever said, 'I'm sorry,' but we both knew. The anger was over. I walked away with an almost indescribable sense of peace. I hope he felt it, too. Jesus was right," the clergyman said. "Resentment is just too heavy a burden to carry around."

I asked, "So, how's the other guy now? Over the years since that encounter, what has your friendship with him been like?"

The minister answered, "Oh, I haven't seen or spoken to him since."

Did those two men forgive one another? In all likelihood they did. But did they take the next step to accept and embrace one another? Obviously not. Forgiveness appears to be something that was turned inward. They each found inner peace by letting go of the burden of resentment that is just too heavy and uncomfortable to bear. As such, forgiveness is something we do for ourselves. We lay down our inner burden. But "mercy" is something we do solely for the other person.

The author of Ephesians said that God not only forgives us our sins but also goes the next step. God accepts and embraces us as children of the Divine. In fact, God does that even while we are still sinful. Here's how the lesson put it: "But God, who is rich in mercy, out of the great love with which he loved us, even when we were immersed in our sins, made us alive together with Christ . . . by grace you have been saved." In other words, God goes beyond forgiveness to mercy, accepting and embracing us as children, even when we don't deserve it.

There is probably no better illustration of that principle than Jesus' story of the prodigal son. In that parable, the father represents God, and the prodigal represents most of us. The son rejected his father's home and values. He ran away and lived in a totally self-indulgent fashion. But finally, the story says, "he came to himself." He realized what a disaster he'd made of things. So he went back to his dad, head hanging and hat in hand, and said, "I am no longer worthy to be part of your family. But would you be willing to treat me as one of your hired servants?" We understand his request. He was simply asking for forgiveness. But what did his father do? He hugged his son to himself and shouted out to the servants, "Cook the fatted calf. Put a ring on my boy's finger and shoes on his feet. Let's have a party. For this, my son, was dead, and is alive again. He was lost, but now I've got him back!"

"This, my son . . . !" The father did not stop with forgiveness. He extended mercy. He accepted, affirmed, and loved the boy as part of the family in spite of what the young man had done.

Not long ago I had two wonderful meals in the same day. What made each wonderful was not only the cuisine but also the fact that they were eaten in the presence of biblical scholars of renown. It was a privilege simply to be with them, to eavesdrop as they thought aloud of grand ideas and transformative theologies. Though the food was good, it was the conversations that made the day great for me. One thing I found particularly intriguing was a single statement I heard two times that day. Each scholar spoke it. Each time it was articulated almost verbatim. Neither had knowledge of my conversation with the other. One at lunch and the other at dinner said to me, "No matter how faithful a person may be, from time to time we all stand in need of mercy."

To be honest, that has been the theme song of my life. At age twelve I sensed a call into ministry. The sky did not open, nor did I hear a voice as Paul did on the road to Damascus. But still, at age twelve I knew. I knew why I was alive. I knew why God put me here. I knew my purpose as much as I knew my own name. God had chosen me to be a preacher. But I also knew something else, and I've known ever since: God has strange taste in who is called to do sacred work. Me, of all people! Totally human, often sinful me—just a plain old flesh-and-blood human being with more Achilles heels than I have feet. Why on earth would God call me? After all, I always believed that preachers were practically perfect, and I knew that I was just the opposite. So why did God choose me?

Across all those growing-up years . . . and those high school years . . . and those college years . . . and those seminary and grad school years . . . and all the years since when I have let God down over and over again, why did God keep calling me to do holy work and to preach a life-saving word? There can be only one answer: mercy. At some point, "God, who is rich in mercy, out of the great love with which he loved us, even when we were immersed in our sins" decided to embrace me, affirm me, and choose me to do a work that is sacred.

Why does God love, accept, and use imperfect people like myself? For the same reason that God loved, accepted, and used drunks like Lot and Noah, concubines liked Esther, thieves like Jacob, crooked tax collectors like Zacchaeus, prostitutes like the woman in Simon's house who anointed Jesus with costly perfume, murderers like David, and accomplices to murder like Paul. For the same reason that after Simon Peter denied even knowing him and left him to die, Jesus sought Peter out and called him not once but three times: "Feed my sheep." As Paul wrote, "We have this treasure in earthen vessels." Why is God interested in people like them, and me, and you? The answer is "mercy."

On June 1, 2005, Percy Arrowsmith, 105 years old, and his 100-year-old wife, Florence, celebrated their eightieth anniversary. Percy died two weeks later. They met at their church in Hereford, England. He sang in the choir, and she was a Sunday school teacher. According to *The Guinness Book of World Records*, until his death they held the record for the longest marriage. At their anniversary party, they were asked what was the secret of staying together (and staying in love) for eighty years. Among the things they listed was this: They said that every night before turning out the lights, they would look at each other and acknowledge what had happened that particular day, good or bad. If there had been a problem, they would be honest about how irritated or angry either of them had become with the other. But then they would each repeat the same words: "What happened today is not half as big as the love I feel for you." Then they would kiss good night, turn out the lights, and drift off to sleep in one another's arms. For eighty years, whenever the need was there, they practiced mercy, and mercy kept their love and their relationship alive.

When we turn to God in guilt or sorrow, when we cry out *Kyrie Eleison* ("Lord, have mercy!"), God always answers, "Whatever you have done or failed to do is not half as big as the love I feel for you." And so God keeps choosing us to be children of the Divine and keeps cradling us within the shelter of loving arms.

Reflection

1. Identify three gifts of mercy Christians are called to offer to their neighbors. How does one practice mercy with those who are resistant to it?

_____

_____

_____

_____

2. Identify three ministries of mercy that Christian churches may offer to the world.

_____

_____

_____

_____

3. Contrast the statement of John Wesley, "The world is my parish," to the attitude of some religious people, "This particular local parish is my world."

_____

_____

_____

_____

A Dual Calling

Now when Jesus heard this, he withdrew from there in a boat to a lonely place apart. But when the crowds heard it, they followed him on foot from the towns. As he went ashore he saw a great throng; and he had compassion on them, and healed their sick. When it was evening, the disciples came to him and said, "This is a lonely place, and the day is now over; send the crowds away to go into the villages and buy food for themselves." Jesus said, "They need not go away; you give them something to eat." They said to him, "We have only five loaves here and two fish." And he said, "Bring them here to me." Then he ordered the crowds to sit down on the grass; and taking the five loaves and the two fish he looked up to heaven, and blessed, and broke and gave the loaves to the disciples, and the disciples gave them to the crowds. And they all ate and were satisfied. And they took up twelve baskets full of the broken pieces left over. And those who ate were about five thousand men, besides women and children. Then he made the disciples get into the boat and go before him to the other side, while he dismissed the crowds. (Matthew 14:13-22)

How terrifying the news is:

• Public beheadings
• A woman stoned to death in a town square because of alleged adultery
• Religious intolerance
• Widespread abuse of women based on religion
• Persecution of people because of their sexuality
• Terrorism
• Conflict in the Holy Land waged by various groups of different (but related) faiths who claim that land as their own and whose distrust and hatred of each other run deep
• Other military forces throughout the Mideast threatening to attack, oppress, and destroy
• New weapons that might make those threats come true

• A frightening epidemic for which there is no cure, ravaging a land of
people who are both innocent and impoverished
• Racism that creates deeper chasms between people here in our own nation
• Tax structures that favor the rich and burden the poor
• Widespread distrust of government officials at national and local levels
• Poverty and hunger and homelessness at rates literally never known before

"How terrifying the news is," those people back in the days of Jesus must
have said, because what I just described, word for word, was life in ancient
Israel 2,000 years ago.

Sometimes we think we invented suffering and fear, but the truth
is that the world has always been going to hell on what seemed like the
express track. We just didn't always have the Internet and YouTube, so we
were forced to watch it happen live. Pick an era, and you will read about

• "Wars and rumors of wars"
• Slavery
• Piratism
• The abuse of children and women and the elderly
• Whole nations or cultures being held captive or annihilated by other,
stronger nations and cultures
• Bubonic plague
• Leprosy
• The Inquisition
• The Barbarians
• Napoleon
• World Wars I and II
• The Holocaust
• Hitler
• Stalin
• Idi Amin
• The KKK
• Saddam Hussein
• ISIS
• Boko Haram
• Putin
• Kim Jong-un
• Syria

The world has always been going to hell, and it still is, but by the grace of God it has never gotten there. The truth is, the sorts of horrors that terrify us today have occurred in every day throughout history. But, as noted, we didn't have to watch those atrocities on our laptops (which is somehow a bit more intense than hearing Walter Cronkite tell you about them a few days later). Yes, we have some pretty threatening villains in the morning news nowadays, but in truth there has never been a day in the whole history of the world when there were not threatening villains at every turn. In time, however, all of them and their movements disappeared, and the Goodness and Truth and Love and transforming Power of Jesus Christ live on.

How do we cope, personally and individually, with a frightening world, the very kind of world people have always had to cope with? Matthew's Gospel gives us a good hint.

Matthew says that Jesus "withdrew to a quiet place." He spent time there alone in prayer, in silence, in spiritual renewal, and in physical rest. Then, the story says, he was better able to deal with the stressful world in which he lived, especially with five thousand needy people who stood before him, "harassed and helpless, like sheep without a shepherd." They were sick, frightened, possessed by demons, depressed, hungry, lonely, without love. Someone had to be there for them, had to be strong for them, and had to be hopeful and helpful for them. And Jesus knew he was that someone. He also knew that you cannot give to others what you do not possess. You cannot be strong for others if you have allowed yourself to become weak. And so, before dealing with the crowd, "he withdrew to a quiet place." Then he came down and fed them, and then he withdrew again (to replenish and recoup because he knew that yet another crowd would be waiting around the next corner).

My wife and I and a few friends were in Israel not long ago. We stood one afternoon on the top of a mountain. It was wind-blown and desolate. St. George's Monastery is carved into the side of the mountain, hundreds of feet above a valley and hundreds of feet below the spot where we stood. The place overlooks "the Valley of the Shadow." It is so quiet that you can hear the wind whistle and sing. There are no other sounds at all. Absolutely none. And, unless a tour bus arrives, there are no people. It is utterly isolated. It is one of the spots many scholars believe the Bible was talking about when it said, "He withdrew to a quiet place." Jesus would go there, or a place like it, for solitude and silence, to be totally alone with his God and with his thoughts.

Near the foot of that mountain is a village. That's where Jesus would return when his sabbatical was over. *Retreat and then return.* He needed refreshment and renewal, and then he was able to serve, and then he renewed himself again, and then he served again. His ministry was cyclical. Even Jesus did not face his frightening world without the occasional time-out from it. It would be foolish to think we have greater strength than he did.

The late Dr. Charles Allen was for many years pastor of a fifteen-thousand-member church in Houston, Texas, and he was also a prolific author. He worked tirelessly every day from early morning to late night, but by his own admission he did not always work intelligently. He did not pace himself. The time came when he was hospitalized. Doctors thought he was suffering from heart disease. It turned out, not surprisingly, that he simply had complete physical exhaustion. While Dr. Allen was lying in a hospital bed, hardly able to move, an old friend, also a preacher, came through the door. He walked across the room, stood beside Dr. Allen's bed, looked at his friend for a long, silent moment, and then spoke. "He maketh me to lie down," he said.

Jesus understood that. He understood that in order to tend to a troubled world, first he had to tend to his own life, so "he withdrew to a quiet place." That's the first principle for facing the world we live in: *take care of yourself.*

Do things that bring you joy, or do nothing at all, if that's what you need from time to time. Go to a movie or read a book. In our neighborhood, walk through Central Park or down Jones Beach, go to the Garden for a ball game or to the Barclay Center for a concert. In your city, there are parks and places just as calming. Find them, and spend time there. Jesus provided the model for that. If you do not occasionally take care of yourself, in time there will not be any essential self left with which to take care of anybody else. Take care of you.

There is a second principle: *take care of your world.* Jesus retreated to the mountain, but he didn't build his home there. He restored his strength in order to be strong for the world that needed him.

How do we do that? I receive e-mails from all over the country asking that question. They don't write because they think Michael Brown is a genius with all the answers. Usually they write because they still associate Marble Collegiate Church with positive thinking and are finding it hard to remain positive in a world like ours. So the e-mails come, asking, "Where do I find hope? How do I keep from giving up? How can one person like me possibly make a difference in a world like this?" And I always answer,

"PRAY." To the cynical or naïve, that may sound like a weak or passive answer. But people of faith understand that few things on earth are stronger or more powerful than prayer. I tell them to pray for three things: (1) Pray that God will do what God has always done. In times of global fear across the ages, people prayed, and eventually all the Lenins and Amins and Hitlers disappeared, and people like Gandhi and Mandela and Mother Teresa and Martin Luther King, Jr. prevailed. So pray that God will do what God has always done. (2) Pray for the strength, courage, and hope to take one step at a time and live one day at a time. Jesus taught, "Sufficient for each day are the troubles thereof" (Matt 6:34). Just pray, "Today, God, though I would not hide my head in the sand, let me see that there are still blessings, still reasons for hope, and still good things in a bad world. Give me the strength I need to make it through today." (3) Pray for a vision of one thing you can do to make a bad world a little better. Just one thing. Let me tell you what that looks like.

I visited with a friend not long ago. He is well into his eighties. He has maintained the same practice for sixty years. He says it's part of what keeps him young inside, no matter what his body says to the contrary. He uses the funniest language: "Every September," he says, "I get pregnant with a new baby." Yes, he is a man. And no, you have not seen his story on the cover of *The Enquirer*. His "new baby" every year is a new project, a new cause that makes life better in his community. During summers, he has a beach house where he and his family vacationed when his children were small. Now, he spends most of each summer there with grandchildren and great-grandchildren. But during his professional life and now during his retirement, when September comes he finds a new baby. And for nine months he carries it. He commits himself to it. Some years it might be a program or project at his church, a beautiful little two-hundred-member congregation that sits high atop a hill over a small winding river. With limited funds, the church relies on volunteers to get almost everything done. Whenever the church has a project that excites him, it becomes his new baby. Sometimes his Lions Club has an initiative he finds inspiring, or a local school tries to do something helpful for hungry or marginalized or special needs children, or an agency like The Salvation Army or his community's Senior Center needs his help.

No matter the cause, every September, he designates nine months for his "new baby." He knows he cannot do all things for all people, but that's never stopped him from doing something for some people. He frequently says, "I can't fix the whole world, but I can keep my little corner of it tidy."

Every September for sixty years he has been finding that "new baby," and his small town is different because of it. Literally his whole community is better and stronger because that one man has faithfully kept his one commitment. He said (and I believe him) that it keeps him young inside.

Do you want to become young inside? Fresh? Energized? Do you want to find life that makes you excited to get out of bed in the morning? And, though you may not be able to solve all the world's ills, are you willing to make your little corner of it brighter and better? Whether or not it's September, maybe the time is right to get yourself a new baby—a new cause to champion, a new work to do, a new service to render, a new way to have a positive impact on a troubled world. None of us can do everything, but all of us can do something. Find that something, that one special cause or issue that needs attention, and throw yourself into it. If we all did that, then this world that seems terrifying might become transformed.

Jesus "withdrew to a quiet place," to take care of himself, his needs, and his soul, but he didn't build his house there. Once his strength was restored, he came back down the mountain to do something for people who had no strength of their own. That's not a bad model for any of us to follow.

Reflection

1. In what sense(s) can self-care be a sacred responsibility?

_____

_____

_____

_____

2. Name three things that bring you a sense of joy or peace.

_____

_____

_____

_____

3. How can an individual contribute to creating a more just or peaceful world?

_____

_____

_____

_____

Empathy

Rejoice with those who rejoice, weep with those who weep. Live in harmony with one another; do not be haughty, but associate with the lowly; never be conceited. (Romans 12:15-16)

Paul indicated that most of us perceive certain spiritual gifts as more visible, more powerful, and maybe even more important than others. He referred to that when he wrote, "If the ear should say, 'Because I'm not an eye, surely I don't matter as much . . . .'" In Romans 12, he lists some of the more famous, prominent spiritual gifts: prophecy, service, teaching, and acts of mercy, and if we couple that with the similar and famous passage in 1 Corinthians 12, he adds things like "speaking in tongues . . . and gifts of administration [keeping the church organized and afloat]." These are all undeniably important and impressive gifts. But, whereas the Romans 12 passage begins with the list, it doesn't end there. If we keep reading, Paul lists additional endowments from God. Unfortunately, too often we tend to stop reading Romans 12 after about the ninth verse. But in truth, the entire chapter is about spiritual gifts, and if we stick with it, we find an intriguing two-verse section about the gift of empathy, not merely of feeling "for" another person but, indeed, feeling "with" them.

In fact, that word ("with") shows up frequently in verses 15 and 16: "Rejoice *with* those who rejoice . . . Weep *with* those who weep . . . Live in harmony *with* one another . . . Associate *with* the lowly." Four times in two brief verses, Paul uses a single word that precludes the possibility of paternalism, that moves us from merely ministering *to* people to actually standing in solidarity *with* people.

Near a subway entrance on Lexington Avenue, a young girl (late teens or early twenties) was seated on a sidewalk. It was a bitterly cold day, and she was not adequately dressed for it. Beside her was a cardboard, hand-printed sign. At her feet was an empty coffee cup for donations. The sign read, "Homeless, please help." I don't know what her story was or how she wound up there. She was just a kid who, one would think, ought to have been home somewhere with parents looking after her or maybe in a dorm preparing for exams and making weekend plans with her friends. Instead, she sat cold and vulnerable on a busy New York City sidewalk. I stopped, reached into my wallet, and pulled out a dollar. A woman in front of me did the same. What caught my interest was the brief exchange between that woman and the young girl. As she dropped the bill into the girl's cup, the woman asked, "How are you doing out here, young lady? Are you safe? Do you have anyone?" The girl looked up and answered, "Thank you. You're the first person all day who has asked about me." It's easy to give money and is incredibly important to do so. It is vital to restoring life and hope to those who are temporarily down and out. But that woman near the subway entrance went beyond donating "to" someone. Instead, she took a moment to stand in the cold of the world "with" someone.

Paul lists several ways in which we witness the gift of empathy being lived out. One, he says, is this: "We weep with those who weep." Probably that's not too difficult most of the time. We read of an elderly man who was mugged on the streets of our city recently. He was just walking alone, carrying two grocery bags, making his way back to his tiny apartment where he lives by himself. It was all caught on camera. Out of nowhere, two young hoodlums appeared. They stole his wallet, which contained almost nothing, and then they beat him severely. The poor man almost died. We read of a five-year-old child taken to Bellevue a few days ago, an innocent little child, whom they feared had contracted Ebola. Thank God that was not the case, but for a few days until the real diagnosis was confirmed, the whole city sat on the edge of our seats waiting and praying. We hear the story of that homeless girl near the subway entrance on Lexington Avenue. Most of us feel touched by these stories and countless others like them. Our eyes grow misty. Maybe we are even moved to do something, to donate something, or at least to pray. Not to be vain but just to be honest, most of us are touched and moved when we witness human pain or suffering.

But Paul also says the spiritual gift of empathy means "We rejoice with those who rejoice," and he adds, "[so] never be conceited." That characteristic ("rejoicing with those who rejoice") is often less common and usually more difficult because it means not allowing our egos to be threatened by someone else's good fortune.

A prominent television personality confessed some time ago on a talk show, "I always resent it a bit when a colleague receives an award." I have known clergy like that. If they hear another minister being complimented for his or her preaching, they will tell you immediately the great reviews they receive on their sermons. Or, if they hear about a sister church that is growing, they will quickly tell you how full their sanctuary is every Sunday. Their vanity cloaks but cannot quite disguise their personal insecurities. Paul says it is a sign of Christian spirituality when we are able to celebrate another person's good fortune and to realize that just because God blesses them doesn't mean God has failed to bless us. "We rejoice with those who rejoice." It takes a mature spirit to do that.

Paul also says, "Live in harmony with one another." Does that mean that in order to be empathetic we have to agree with other people all time? Of course not. Some people articulate ideas with which we cannot, in good faith, agree. To "live in harmony" means, instead, that whether or not we agree with another person, we at least respect them. And what does respect have to do with empathy? Consider the following example (all of us could offer dozens more).

An out-of-state viewer used to web stream our worship services every Sunday morning and every Wednesday night. She was also faithful in watching our Thursday virtual services. She died a year or so ago. Periodically I would receive a brief e-mail from her thanking me for a sermon or bragging on the music. She could be endearingly warm and gracious. But there were other times (not as often, but once in a while) when an e-mail would come, usually out of the blue, and she would be livid about a sermon I had preached. Her attack on me would be scathing, accusing me of being political or on the wrong side of some issue. Occasionally she would even write, "How could you say something so stupid?" Those e-mails were always hostile and vitriolic, frequently including rants and raves that were racist or homophobic, and most of the time accusing me of saying things I had actually not even hinted at in a sermon, let alone expressed. I would go back and read through the manuscript or listen to the tape, and what she was angry about simply wasn't there!

How did I respond? Did her political views convert me? Of course not. They were preposterous. Did I enter into an e-mail debate, trying to convince her? What a waste of time that would be. Instead, I sent a brief e-mail, usually saying, "Thanks for listening to the sermon and for responding. I appreciate the fact that we can disagree on issues while still seeking to serve the same God. Tell me, how have you been doing lately?" Over the years, the woman had lost both a husband and later a child in tragic accidents. She lived with deep, painful wounds. For the most part she had managed to cope. But sometimes the pains would resurface, and one of the stages of grief is anger. She couldn't dispel that anger toward her employer, or she would have been fired. She couldn't vent it at her friends, because most of them would have walked away. But she had to express it to someone, and a preacher in another city whom she would never meet face to face was an easy target. So when the target would reply, "Tell me, how have you been doing lately?," another e-mail would arrive. Only this time it would not be angry, political, or hostile. Instead, it was always an open, honest outpouring of all the grief and fear and hurt she carried around inside. For me in those moments, "living in harmony" with someone like that did not mean agreeing with her, but it did mean respecting her, listening to her without being sucked into an argument, and trying to understand the personal pains that were the source of her hostile actions. She wasn't a bad person. She was a wounded person. In her more reasonable times, when no anger was expressed, we were able to communicate positively about faith and race and gender and environment and church and all sorts of things. And maybe that was possible because in those other moments, by God's grace and not by my nature, I tried to offer not retaliation but empathy. "Rejoice *with* those who rejoice . . . Weep *with* those who weep . . . Live in harmony *with* one another."

Exercising the spiritual gift of empathy means not only feeling *for* people but also feeling *with* people, not only making gifts but also making room, not only offering charity but also offering time and compassion and a listening ear. May we learn to be empathetic.

Reflection

1. What is the difference between "sympathy" and "empathy"?

_____

_____

_____

_____

2. "You do not have to like people to perform deeds of love for them."[9] Do you think this is true or untrue? If true, how do we rise above the behavior of another in determining how we will behave toward them?

_____

_____

_____

_____

3. Do you think personality is more a matter of genetics or environment? Whichever you believe, does it effect how we are called to treat others? Explain.

_____

_____

_____

_____

Priorities

"You blind guides, straining out a gnat and swallowing a camel! Woe to you, scribes and Pharisees, hypocrites! For you cleanse the outside of the cup and of the plate, but inside they are full of extortion and rapacity. You blind Pharisee! First cleanse the inside of the cup and of the plate, that the outside also may be clean. Woe to you, scribes and Pharisees, hypocrites! For you are like whitewashed tombs, which outwardly appear beautiful, but within they are full of dead men's bones and all uncleanness. So you also outwardly appear righteous to men, but within you are full of hypocrisy and iniquity." (Matthew 23:24-28)

A familiar statement says, "Very few of us are ever swallowed by whales. Instead, most of us are nibbled to death by minnows." Or, as another proverb puts it, "The devil is in the details."

Who would argue that life is often dominated by details, by little things that nibble away at our time and energy like minnows? The question is, how do we keep this from happening? How do we protect ourselves from being so overwhelmed by a thousand little things that we never get around to the handful of other things that really matter? How do we answer the biblical calling to put first things first? And it is truly a biblical calling as indicated by the words of Jesus in the Sermon on the Mount: "Seek ye first the kingdom of God," and then everything else will fall into place as it should (Matt 6:33).

Retired United Methodist Bishop Bevel Jones used to say frequently, "The main thing is to keep the main thing the main thing!"

A time-management consultant on a morning TV news show talked about interruptions in the workplace. She said one key to success in business is to enter the office every morning and ask, "What is the primary task before me today? What is the most important thing I have been hired to do?" Then, she said, our focus should be on addressing that task, and we should tend to lesser tasks or interruptions only after the primary task is accomplished. "Otherwise," she said, "an endless barrage of little things will get in the way of the main thing."

So how do we do it? How do we keep our lives from being nibbled to death by minnows? How do we keep the main thing the main thing?

Here is what I think it looks like for clergy, based on my forty years of life in this profession. My first callings from God are to preach, to teach, and to envision ministry. When I became senior minister of Marble Collegiate Church, I took part in the tradition of The Reformed Church in America, which has a Service of Installation using language that identified me as a "teaching pastor." I was not installed as a CEO, though every minister must attend to administrative tasks and do so from a seat of bestowed leadership. I was not installed as a fund-raiser, though stewardship is always a priority for a local church pastor. I was not installed as an HR official, though ministry to and management of staff is a real role of a clergyperson's work and one that should not be ignored or dismissed. I was not installed as an apologist for the system who spends most of the time going from one meeting to the next, though the importance of tending to the affairs of the organization cannot be minimized. I was installed as teaching pastor. And primary to that role, as I understand it, is the function of faithfully preaching the good news of God's redemptive entry into the world through the person of Jesus Christ. A recognized responsibility articulated during my installation was to connect that timeless message of faith to the needs and issues of the people who sit in our pews or tune in on their televisions or laptops in this specific day and age. They come to us hoping for a word of faith that can help them move from one day to the next, and I am called to do my best to provide it. Contrary to popular belief (or how a sermon may sometimes sound), preachers do not just stand up, open their mouths, and begin to talk.

A certain minister apparently decided he could do that (just stand up without preparation and preach). He began to imagine that all the hours spent in preparing sermons were wasted and were, in fact, an expression of lack of faith in the presence of God during the preaching event. "After all," he thought, "God is the real preacher. I'm just the mouthpiece. It is almost unfaithful for me to work on sermons and not give God the chance to say what God wants to say. So I'm not going to do that anymore." All that week the preacher had a great time. The hours he ordinarily spent studying, writing, editing, rewriting, and memorizing, he spent playing golf instead. He was on the course five times that week. He felt renewed and refreshed. Then came Sunday morning. When he entered the pulpit, before opening his mouth as he stood to preach, he bowed his head and prayed, "O Lord, what do you want me to tell these people today?" In the silence he heard the Lord's voice answer, "Why don't you tell them how to putt?"

Preparing to preach with any sort of intelligibility is an exacting and time-consuming task. George Buttrick, the late, great minister of Madison Avenue Presbyterian Church in our city, and later Professor of Preaching at Southern Seminary in Louisville, instructed his students that every minute in the pulpit should represent an hour in the study. Though that may be somewhat exaggerated, the point remains that one cannot ignore the importance of being prepared.

Buttrick was correct in educating his students that sermons do not just magically happen. They require preparation time—and lots of it. Most weeks in our church, I preach a Sunday morning sermon, a Wednesday evening sermon, and a Thursday noon virtual (web only) sermon. Even at 60 percent of Buttrick's estimated time of preparation, I ordinarily put in between thirty-five and forty hours of sermon preparation before even getting around to the other tasks of ministry: pastoral care, staff management, blog writing, and attendance at far too many meetings. That seems like a lot of work. But it is work that cannot be short-changed. We cannot allow other things to intrude on it or diminish its importance. Every preacher alive understands that every week there will be countless causes impinging upon our primary calling. So we must remain diligent in putting first things first, lest we cheat both church and the One who called us. I have a friend, an outstanding preacher, who every morning at 8:00 places a sign on his office door. It simply reads, "If someone died, please knock." It is his way of saying that he will attend to first things first, and his church members are rewarded for that. Almost unanimously they applaud his discipline of keeping the main thing the main thing.

Enough about preachers. All that was merely illustrative, an attempt to open an avenue of thought so that you can reflect on your own life, your own priorities, your own sense of calling, and how to deal with the myriad lesser issues that would detract from your primary responsibility. What does it mean to you to put first things first? What does it mean to you to prioritize in life so that your time, your energy, and your soul do not get nibbled to death by minnows?

I read about a mother and father who became co-chairs of a community bridge association. They served a two-year stint in that capacity. The association sponsored bridge tournaments and bridge clubs all over town, teaching the craft to countless people who wanted to learn and raising considerable amounts of money for charitable organizations. It was fun work, but it was by no means merely frivolous work. That couple, as co-chairs, attended some related event on an average of four nights per week. During their time in office, their teenaged daughter began to distribute illegal drugs out of their home. Obviously, mom and dad were rarely home, so they simply did not notice. But they did notice one night when they arrived at their house and saw blue lights flashing, then watched as their daughter was led in handcuffs to a squad car. She went to jail because of the unwise choices she had made. No one, including her parents, made those choices for her. And yet, to a certain extent at least, because her parents had let lesser things take precedence over the main thing, their daughter was vulnerable.

Years ago, a young man came to my office in tears. He reported how he had gone home unexpectedly one afternoon and found his wife in a romantic situation with a neighbor. He came to see me emotionally devastated. But, surprisingly, his anger was not so much directed at his wife or his neighbor as at himself. He told me that for five years he had sought to cultivate professional relationships that would move him up the corporate ladder. So every afternoon, weather permitting, he played golf with his supervisors from the office. Even in bad weather, they still went to the club, drank whiskey sours, and played cards till bedtime. Monday through Friday, he stayed with them on the course or over the card table, substituting the club grill for home and family. He told his story in tears and confessed, "I treated my wife like a single mother for so long that she obviously began to feel single." He had let lesser issues take precedence over the main thing.

It is not that other things in life are evil or unimportant. But when we fail to prioritize, when we fail to put first things first, we are gambling with the essence of our very lives. We're allowing ourselves to be nibbled to death by minnows.

Jesus knew that this happens, sometimes even among good and well-meaning people. The Gospel of Matthew says he uttered challenges to Pharisees. Not to thieves and ax murderers, mind you, but to Pharisees. Church leaders. The most religious people you could ever hope to meet back in those days. People who not only strictly observed the Ten Commandments but also observed more than six hundred other religious rules and regulations.

A minister was involved in a conversation with a notorious man in his church. The man was a Christmas-and-Easter church person who spent the rest of the time leading an unbelievably "colorful" life. So the minister asked him, "How can you be so unconcerned about keeping the Ten Commandments?" The man answered, "Preacher, I am not unconcerned. At one time or another in my life, I've kept all of them!"

The Pharisees would have fainted dead away at that. No one was more concerned with living righteously than they were. But they were the very people Jesus challenged at the point of their priorities. "You blind guides," he said. "You strain at a gnat and swallow a camel! Woe to you, scribes and Pharisees, hypocrites! You [worry about rules and regulations on how to] cleanse the outside of the cup and plate, but inside [you hardly even notice things like] extortion and greed." They had failed in their calling to keep the main thing the main thing. They allowed lesser issues to crowd out the issues that ultimately mattered most.

Like those Pharisees, most "religious" people are not immune to doing that sort of thing. We say that Jesus is first for us (as well he should be), but our actions sometimes fail to back up our words. It is too easy to let good things get in the way of the main thing.

How many faithful religious folks who attend their centers of worship every week feel that they do not have enough time to take on a job in the church, even though they have ample time to work for their civic club?

How many of us feel that we do not have enough time to allot even a few minutes each day for prayer or study of Scripture, but we have more than enough time for watching *Monday Night Football* or *The Voice*?

How many of us allocate more money each year to our alma mater or country club or wardrobes or vacation plans than we give to our churches or local charitable organizations, and it never even occurs to us that when we write our checks, God observes our priorities?

Someone told me of being so moved by the plight of the victims of Hurricane Irene that she sent $100 to the Red Cross. In the same conversation, she told me of hiring a new ballet teacher for "only $4,000 a year." If ballet were her career, then what she said would be absolutely understandable. Ballet, however, is merely one of her numerous hobbies. What we do with our possessions and our time reveals our priorities.

"Woe to you, scribes and Pharisees, hypocrites! You strain at a gnat and swallow a camel!" Do not misinterpret. Your civic club and TV shows and country clubs and alma maters and hobbies are worthy of your investments, whether of money or of time. But sometimes even "religious people" forget their primary callings and allow good things to take precedence over God's things.

That advice, obviously, is pertinent not only for individual Christians but also for congregations. We must remain diligent never to major in minors, never to become absorbed to the point of being obsessed with issues that are not "the main thing."

Peter Drucker used to teach with clarity and power that the core purpose of a nonprofit institution is to change lives. Whatever church a person may attend, how often is that topic central when your committees meet? Instead, we spend most of our time talking about important things like budgets, governance models, and facility issues and often omitting the main thing: *What are we doing to transform human lives?* Sometimes, said Jesus, even good people, religious people, "strain at gnats and swallow camels."

Exiting a restaurant with some church members not long ago, we spotted a sign near the door. It said, "Success does not happen by accident." Jesus said that to the Pharisees. Bevel Jones said it to his audiences. Life says it eloquently and powerfully when it comes to our professions, our relationships, and even our faith: success, happiness, and fulfillment do not come by accident. They come only when we say yes to our primary calling—and that is always to keep the main thing the main thing.

Reflection

1. In your personal life, identify pressing matters that often distract you from crucial matters. Identify issues in the lives of churches that sometimes distract from urgent and authentic ministry.

_____

_____

_____

_____

2. Discuss the roles of prayer, Scripture, and conversation with people of faith in adequately prioritizing your life or the life of a local church.

_____

_____

_____

_____

3. At the end of your life's journey, what few things do you want to be able to look back and say about yourself? How can you make that happen?

_____

_____

_____

_____

Counting on Christ

Jesus Christ is the same yesterday and today and forever. Do not be led away by diverse and strange teachings; for it is well that the heart be strengthened by grace, not by foods, which have not benefited their adherents. (Hebrews 13:8-9)

To a great extent I admire politicians on both sides of the aisle. Washington, Jefferson, Lincoln, FDR, and Eisenhower were politicians, just like Churchill and de Gaulle and Meir and Thatcher and Bhutto. America and the rest of the world are forever in their debt. Most politicians are civil *servants*, and they deserve both our prayers and our respect.

That being said, just like clergy and virtually everyone else, sometimes some politicians can be silly. In 2004 a man ran for office in my home state. Apparently he did not think his constituents understood the English language very well because he campaigned as "a bold conservative." There is honor in being bold, and there is honor in being conservative—but according to *Webster's Dictionary* you can't be both. You have to choose bold or conservative. Either one is fine, but you've got to choose. His campaign insulted the voters who apparently recognized his error and elected somebody else. His ad was *inconsistent*.

That campaign slogan reminds us of the oxymorons we use all the time, as if they actually made sense:

• A fine mess
• Perfectly awful
• Hot chili
• Inside out
• Pretty ugly
• Act naturally
• Resident alien
• Same difference
• Sanitary landfill
• Airline food

We accept these phrases and use them, no matter how inconsistent they may be. And we use them not only in our speech but also in our personal philosophies of life when we embrace inconsistencies. Our purpose at this point is not to debate hot topics. But let's use one of those topics to illustrate how inconsistent we sometimes are. Many people call themselves "pro-life" but still support capital punishment. How pro-life is that? Many others consider themselves "pro-choice" but still oppose capital punishment (the right of collective individuals called the "state" to choose to end a life). How pro-choice is that? If you're serious when you preach about the sanctity of life, does that not by definition include both a fetus and a prisoner on death row? Or, if you're serious when you preach about freedom of choice, must that not apply philosophically to both a particular individual and also to the collective individuals that we call a "state"? This is not to argue for or against either of those positions. It is simply to point out the obvious: that most of us are philosophically inconsistent.

We humans are like that. How many folks never know whether their employer is going to be pleasant or hateful on a particular day? In all likelihood, it depends on what happened at home during breakfast or the night before. One day your boss treats you with respect and kindness and the next day treats you disrespectfully and inhumanely. Thus, each time you walk into the office, your stomach is tied in knots because you work for someone who is inconsistent.

Of course, it is far too easy to point an accusing finger at the rest of the world. The author of Hebrews pointed out that even members of the infant Christian church were profoundly inconsistent at times. Sometimes we still are.

A seminary classmate of mine, Robert, served a beautiful church on the coast of North Carolina. During one summer vacation I stopped by to visit him, and he told me about a man he knows in Tennessee. The man is actively involved in a church and has held virtually every leadership position it has to offer. He is also a mega-wealthy businessman who years ago made a commitment that he would do anything necessary to make a lot of money. Not long ago, he contacted my friend and said that when the time comes, he wants my friend to officiate at his funeral. As they talked about what he wanted done, the man said to Robert, "I want two songs sung, one Christian and one secular. The hymn really describes my faith," the man said, "and the other song describes my life." The hymn he chose was "Have Thine Own Way, Lord," and the secular song was "I Did It My

Way." Apparently he did not recognize the inconsistency in those musical selections.

The author of Hebrews talked about Christians who ignore the poor, the imprisoned, and the mistreated; Christians who are unfaithful in marriage, who worship money instead of God, or who fail to pray for their leaders; Christians who worship both God *and* false idols; Christians who preach grace but establish and seek to enforce rigid rules. In short, he wrote that even followers of Christ sometimes say one thing and do another. They/we are inconsistent. And he echoed the question that haunts us: In a world like this where even disciples do not always live up to what they proclaim, is there anything or anyone we can actually count on? The author continued with what is perhaps the most famous phrase he ever wrote: "Jesus Christ [is] the same yesterday, today, and forever" (Heb 13:8).

If that verse is true, and if Jesus promised "I will be with you always" (Matt 28:20), then he will not change his mind and abandon us when the tough times come.

If that verse is true, and if Jesus promised "Neither then do I condemn you" (John 8:11), then he will not change his mind when we fail or sin or drop the ball. He will not cast us off as if we were criminals.

If that verse is true, and if Jesus promised "I have come that you might have life abundant" (John 10:10), then he will not change his mind and decide he would rather see us suffer instead.

If that verse is true, and if Jesus promised "In my Father's house are many rooms, and I go to prepare a place for you" (John 14:2), then he will not change his mind and let death be the end of everything.

"Jesus Christ is the same yesterday, today, and forever." This means that he can be trusted, that he is divinely consistent. He doesn't promise one thing and then deliver something else. He is as good as his word. In this world where "The only thing constant is change,"[10] Jesus is the exception. He does not change the rules on us. He is the one thing we can count on!

Ron Newhouse, a delightful preacher and daily devotional writer, tells of a woman in his church who faced serious surgery and was understandably frightened. Who wouldn't be? The night before she entered the hospital, a neighbor dropped by for a visit, just to be with her and offer comfort and encouragement. The neighbor asked, "How are you doing?" to which the woman confessed, "I am terrified. Every time I think about the surgery, I am scared to death." Her friend responded, "Do you know how many times the Bible says either 'Fear not' or 'Be not afraid'?" The frightened woman said that she had no idea. Her neighbor continued,

"The Bible uses those phrases exactly three hundred and sixty-five times. Not three hundred and sixty-four. Not three hundred and sixty-six. But three hundred and sixty-five times, once for every day of the year. It's as if God reminds us every morning, 'I'm still here. I was here yesterday and the day before that. I'm here today. I'll be here tomorrow and the day after that, too.'"[11] Whenever we need him, Jesus promised, "I will be with you always!" He is divinely consistent.

A retired United Methodist Bishop, commenting on the formative influences of his life, said, "My father never varied in how he treated my brother, my sister, and me. He always expected nothing less than the best from us, and he always forgave us when we failed to live up to those expectations." The strength he received from his father was a sense of consistency—both in moral principles and also in grace. Jesus is like that. "My father never varied in how he treated my brother, my sister, and me." Likewise, Jesus never varies in how he treats us, both in his call to moral principles *and* in his willingness to extend grace. He never varies in his love for us, his presence with us, his expectations of us, his kindness to us, or his passion about us.

In a world where "the only thing constant is change," if we are looking for something to count on, that something is Someone. "Jesus Christ is the same yesterday, today, and for ever," wrote the author of Hebrews. Simply put, Jesus never varies in how he loves us or how he treats us. His presence, grace, and compassion are divinely consistent.

Reflection

1. If Jesus were present in our community today, what public issues do you think he would champion?

_____

_____

_____

_____

2. If Jesus were present in our community today, what public or church practices do you think he would challenge?

_____

_____

_____

_____

3. In a constantly changing world, what is your personal understanding of the text, "Jesus Christ [is] the same yesterday, today, and forever"?

_____

_____

_____

_____

The Community of Faith

Richard Wilke concluded his important book, *And Are We Yet Alive?* with this statement: "The Holy Spirit can empower us [the church] to speak in all the languages of the world, can enable all women and men, old and young, of every race and nation to be inviting witnesses of peace, and can enflame the mission of Jesus Christ to save a lost and lonely world."[12]

Were his words merely wishful thinking? I am convinced they were more than that. I think his words form a model of appropriate thinking for those of us who practice faith. Perhaps they even constitute a goal (or *the* goal?) toward which to aspire. Most of us experience faith in two ways: cognitively (individually, prayerfully, meditatively) and corporately (in community with other believers). One way devoid of the other is, to use Ben Franklin's analogy of the dynamics of marriage, like "half a pair of scissors." Whereas your prayers cannot take the place of my own life of prayer and meditation and your acts of service cannot compensate for my own lethargy or inactivity, it is undeniable that our acts of discipleship together go further and accomplish more than either of our acts alone. And whereas I may experience God in solitude, creeds and choral acts of praise and sacraments and calls to systemic-transforming action occur with greatest impact where two or three or hundreds or thousands are gathered together in Jesus' name.

The nature of church has been changing for two thousand years (understandably, even as the nature of society has likewise been changing), but the church itself has not ceased to be an institution of significance and unique power. Jesus himself promised that "the gates of hell [the powers of evil] would not prevail" against the church (Matt 16:18). It needs to be noted, of course, that when making that promise he was also placing the future the future of church into human hands. He was with his disciples at Caesarea Philippi. Simon Peter had just confessed Jesus as Messiah. And Jesus said that upon Peter's confession, made by a human and extended in word and deed from human to human, the church would be built.

You and I are the contemporary caretakers of the institution Jesus established. In fact, more than merely being caretakers, we are church crafters. We are called not merely to protect an ancient foundation but also to build upon it.

Consider a few biblical statements, assessments, and challenges about church and what is required to move a historic fellowship into a healthy future.

Sabbath

At that time Jesus went through the grain fields on the sabbath; his disciples were hungry, and they began to pluck heads of grain and to eat. But when the Pharisees saw it, they said to him, "Look, your disciples are doing what is not lawful to do on the sabbath." He said to them, "Have you not read what David did, when he was hungry, and those who were with him: how he entered the house of God and ate the bread of the Presence, which it was not lawful for him to eat nor for those who were with him, but only for the priests? Or have you not read in the law how on the sabbath the priests in the temple profane the sabbath, and are guiltless? I tell you, something greater than the temple is here. And if you had known what this means, 'I desire mercy, and not sacrifice,' you would not have condemned the guiltless. For the Son of Man is lord of the sabbath." (Matthew 12:1-8)

I ran across a list of quotes recently about the "under-energized" population. Let me share a few with you:

• "Today is the first day of the rest of my life. Of course, tomorrow will be, too—so I'll wait to get started till then."
• "If they ever give out an award for laziness, I'll send someone to pick it up for me."
• "Laziness is the mother of all bad habits. But then, she is a mother, so we need to respect her."
• "If something is more than five feet away, I really didn't need it anyhow."
• And this one from Bill Gates: "I always choose a lazy person to do a difficult job because he will find a quick and easy way to get it done."

Why include these particular quotes? Because I know a man who is type A personality times two. He is hyper, wired, always busy, and he sometimes says, "The whole idea of Sabbath was just some religious person's excuse for being lazy!"

What do you think? What is behind the historic idea of Sabbath/ *Shabbat*? Apparently a lot of people agree with my hyper friend. A recent survey posed this question: "What does the word 'Sabbath' mean to you?" Overwhelmingly, the first reply was, "The Sabbath is a day off from work." Most of the answers provided to the question had hardly any religious connotation at all.

The first hit of the Bangles, the groundbreaking female rock band from the 1980s, was a song called "Manic Monday." It was about the dread of returning to work on Monday morning, going back to the office, back to the desk, and back to the grind. One line in the refrain said, "I wish it were Sunday. That's my fun day!" For many, that is apparently our understanding of Sabbath.

The idea of Sabbath began as a spiritual Law. In fact, *Shabbat* is the only religious day required by the Ten Commandments. Not Yom Kippur. Not Passover. Not Hanukkah. But in the Law of Moses, believers are commanded to observe the Sabbath, to set aside a day for both personal *and* spiritual renewal. Consider a story found in Matthew's Gospel about the religious understanding of *Shabbat* in the days of Jesus:

> At that time Jesus went through the grain fields on the Sabbath; his disciples were hungry, and they began to pluck heads of grain and to eat. But when the Pharisees saw it, they said to him, "Look, your disciples are doing what is not lawful to do on the Sabbath."

What unlawful thing were the disciples doing? According to the Pharisees, anything that constituted work was unlawful. Picking food was work. All food had to be picked and prepared before the Sabbath began. So when the disciples plucked heads of grain to eat, the Pharisees were convinced that they had broken moral law and offended God.

In the era when I grew up in a small town in the South, our community observed "Blue Laws." Basically, this meant that anything that was not an absolute necessity could not be purchased on Sunday. Pharmacies were open, but only in order to sell medicine, a necessity for those who were sick. If a family member went into the pharmacy to pick up your prescription, they were not allowed to purchase hair spray or toothpaste in addition. For those items, you could return to the store tomorrow. My father was a radio journalist, making him probably one of the more liberal men in town. He had also once worked at a station in New York City, which put him off the liberal chart for some folks in our community. Even so, he and my mother made decisions about what I could and could not do on the Sabbath. If I were too sick to go to church on Sunday morning, then there was no need to feel better on Sunday afternoon because I still would not be allowed to hang out with my friends. And, no matter how often I begged, I was not allowed to attend a movie on Sunday until my senior year in high school when my begging finally wore them down. They relented and permitted me to take a date to a local theater. But there were codicils: First, my parents got to choose the movie. They chose *The Sound of Music*. And, I suspect to keep me from ever asking again, the second requirement was that my parents went to the movie with us!

In our town, without meaning to, we were the Pharisees, people who said the Sabbath is about what you are not allowed to do. But Jesus said it the other way around: "The Sabbath is made for us, and not us for the Sabbath." Jesus understood why the Law was established—not to impose restrictions but to renew and restore the lives and spirits of believers, not to make life more difficult but to allow us to regroup and refresh so that we would have sufficient energy to overcome life's difficulties. To that extent, the Bangles were right. Before we are ready for another "Manic Monday," we need a Sunday, a fun day, a relaxing day to refuel for life's journey.

> He said to them, "Have you not read what David did, when he was hungry, and those who were with him: how he entered the house of God and ate the bread of the Presence, which it was not lawful for him to eat nor for those who were with him, but only for the priests? Or have you not read in the law how on the Sabbath the priests in the temple profane the Sabbath, and are guiltless?"

Again, Jesus underscored the principle that the Sabbath is for you, to feed your needs, to strengthen your life, to "restore your soul." In that sense, Jesus pointed out that there are a variety of ways to observe Sabbath. And, according to this passage from Matthew, not all of them occurred in the temple. The ways to experience Sabbath healing are as diverse as the people who practice them:

• I often find almost unparalleled relaxation and am exposed to undeniable proclamations of Truth by going to the theater.
• My wife tells me she sometimes senses nearness of God in a special way while practicing yoga.

• A friend of mine says that he feels keenly spiritual "beside the still waters" when sailing on his boat.

• St. Francis of Assisi was asked, "If you knew the world would end in an hour, what would you do?" He replied, "I would keep working in my garden," for God is there.

Do not misinterpret me. I am not saying that church is dispensable and we can find God any old place. A man said to a clergy friend of mine, "I can worship God just as well on the golf course." My friend answered, "And when your daughter wants to get married, or your grandbaby needs to be baptized, or you lie in a hospital bed sick and frightened and needing prayer, how does the pro from the golf course work out for you?"

Worship . . . fellowship with Christian friends . . . Christian education . . . small groups . . . organized missions . . . support systems that provide love and hope and principles of faith . . . . All those things and more, I think, make church indispensable. And yet moments exist on days other than Sunday and in places other than church where, in the sounds of silence, we encounter the presence of God and our souls are restored. Whatever those moments are for you, wherever those places may be, here is a suggestion worth considering: Go there more often. Do whatever it is more frequently. Create more opportunities to find Sabbath wherever it uniquely exists for you.

> "I tell you, something greater than the temple is here. And if you had known what this means, 'I desire mercy, and not sacrifice,' you would not have condemned the guiltless. For the Son of Man is lord of the Sabbath."

The leaders of the faith were being unfaithful. Jesus said they were "profaning the Sabbath." That is not something with which we are unfamiliar. We know about tacking God's name onto our evil deeds in an attempt to justify them. The savage, ungodly acts of ISIS, the group contends, are done to honor God. In Matthew's story, what the priests did was not nearly as brutal, but Jesus said it was still ungodly. Why? Because they turned the Sabbath into a burden instead of a blessing, and they did so in God's name. They used rules and rituals to load guilt upon people who were already weary. They told them they were not good enough, they had not done enough, their sacrifices were not great enough. They made religion about Law instead of Love!

And, in fact, it was even worse than that. When Jesus became angry and drove the moneychangers out of the temple, he said it was because they had turned God's "house of prayer" into "a den of thieves" (see Matt 21). Here's what they were doing: Sacrificial doves were required as offerings from those seeking God's favor. The priests also had to declare the doves to be "without blemish." The poor often bought the only doves they could afford from vendors down the street. Those were the same doves as the ones sold in the temple. No difference. But the priests would examine the birds and say, "No. These from the street are not good enough. They are blemished. You must buy one of ours" (which were, of course, incredibly more expensive). And the poor had no choice if they wanted to make their sacrifice. Additionally, they believed that if they didn't, God would judge them, reject them, and even abandon them. So they would hand over every last penny to the priests, sometimes even money they had set aside to buy food for their children. They were robbed ostensibly in order to "keep the Sabbath." Jesus said that is "profane" and that God "desires mercy, not sacrifice." Grace, not doves.

Recently I received a letter from a woman who moved to the West Coast. Years earlier, she had come to NYC more or less to escape a difficult life that included a religiously oppressive and psychologically abusive upbringing. At age twenty, she ran away from that and wound up here. Somewhere along the line, one of my church members told her about our congregation. She said, "I don't do church. My parents forced me to go to church. Church was where I learned that God hates me; home was where I learned my parents felt same." But apparently our congregant wore her down and she finally attended (the first time, reluctantly), then attended again, and again, and again, continuing to be involved for several years until recently moving. In her letter, she described what she found at Marble: acceptance, love free of charge, affirmation that she was God's child and therefore she was good, and the subsequent birth of a sense of self-respect that she had never known before.

It was a long, moving letter. In its conclusion, she wrote these words and gave me permission to share them: "As a child, I dreaded Sundays and being reminded of how sinful I was. In New York, I couldn't wait for Sundays when I would be reminded of how deeply loved I was, even by the very God I had once been taught to fear. What I found on Sundays at Marble was a personal oasis, a healing place, a fountain where I could drink in the truth about God and about myself. Sundays in that church helped me discover the secret to finally enjoy life from Monday through Saturday.

Now, in spite of the miles, every Sunday in my head and in my heart I come back there, and I find that same sense of peace all over again."

She was saying that when she came to church, she discovered "Sabbath"—time and place where God cradled her and comforted her and reassured her that she was good and she was loved. And her whole life has changed because of it.

Maybe the Bangles were right when they sang "Manic Monday." Maybe they knew what Sabbath actually means when they sang, "I wish it were Sunday, that's my fun day." Jesus was not far removed from that when he said, "The Sabbath was made for us, and not us for the Sabbath." It is a time of refreshment and renewal, not a time of burden. It is a time of blessing—a time, as that woman wrote, to drink in the truth about ourselves and about God. And the truth is that you are good, no matter what anyone else has tried to tell you, and God loves you deeply and forever. In that truth we find peace. That's what Sabbath is about. It's what we should be able to find in churches on Sundays and therefore in our hearts Mondays through Saturdays.

Reflection

1. What are the spiritual benefits of Sabbath?

_____

_____

_____

_____

2. What are the physical/emotional benefits of Sabbath?

_____

_____

_____

_____

3. What do you think Jesus meant when he said, "I desire mercy, not sacrifice"?

_____

_____

_____

_____

Coping with Conflict

Therefore, my brethren, whom I love and long for, my joy and crown, stand firm thus in the Lord, my beloved. I entreat Euodia and I entreat Syntyche to agree in the Lord. And I ask you also, true yokefellow, help these women, for they have labored side by side with me in the gospel together with Clement and the rest of my fellow workers, whose names are in the book of life.

Rejoice in the Lord always; again I will say, Rejoice. Let all men know your forbearance. The Lord is at hand. Have no anxiety about anything, but in everything by prayer and supplication with thanksgiving let your requests be made known to God. And the peace of God, which passes all understanding, will keep your hearts and your minds in Christ Jesus.

Finally, whatever is true, whatever is honorable, whatever is just, whatever is pure, whatever is lovely, whatever is gracious, if there is any excellence, if there is anything worthy of praise, think about these things. What you have learned and received and heard and seen in me, do; and the God of peace will be with you. (Philippians 4:1-9)

It's difficult to describe what the Internet has done to the craft of preaching. Since my sermons appear online, I receive letters from all over the world with comments, compliments, and critiques. I deeply appreciate hearing from all who write. By the same token, this new virtual age dictates that what we say from the pulpit must be accurate. Following an illustration I used in a sermon some time ago, I received a letter from a pastor in Mississippi who said, "Let me tell you how that story really went. I am the woman's pastor." Similarly, I received a note from a man in Ohio who wrote, "Thanks for saying all those nice things about me in your sermon last week." I didn't know him and had simply been quoting from a story I read in a magazine. But, after hearing from him, I am glad the things I said sounded accurate and affirming, as he was listening when I told his story. The truth is, most of us preachers pick up an illustration someplace, check its accuracy as well as possible given the context of sermon writing, and then pass it along to our listeners. But now, due to the Internet, when I do so there is always the possibility (even the likelihood) that someone who lived or witnessed the story will contact me with editorial comments. In short, accuracy is always a virtue.

So let me issue a disclaimer before I pass this story along to you. The man who told it to me said, "I *think* this happened in Tacoma, Washington, but I'm not sure." If you are from Tacoma and realize it did not occur there, then I give you my apologies. In any event, my friend told about a civic club meeting in progress in Tacoma (or somewhere in the Pacific northwest), in which the members were debating how to allocate proceeds from their annual fundraising event. There was a difference of opinion between those who wanted to give the money to local charitable projects and others who thought the money should be retained and applied to a renovation project on the club's building. The debate, which became uncharacteristically heated, waged on and on. Fingers were pointed. Friends who had worked side by side on the fund-raiser began to speak unkindly toward one another. While the debate raged, two burglars entered the back room of the building undetected and walked away with every penny of the $8,500 the civic club had raised. While they argued among themselves, they lost their shirts!

That often happens to groups or organizations when conflict overcomes collegiality, when an individual's need to win takes priority over the organization's need to succeed. I frequently refer to the Philippian church because it was, I think, the primary model of what a church is meant to be. And yet, even there it was not Utopia. In the fourth chapter of Philippians, Paul comments on a situation of conflict or competitiveness within that congregation, a situation with the potential to hamper and diminish the vision and mission of the Philippian congregation.

Apparently a disagreement was in progress between two leaders. There is an adage that when churches fight, the devil takes a holiday. Paul wanted to make sure that did not happen in Philippi. Two women who had labored side by side for Christ and with Paul obviously had a significant difference of opinion about some issue. And rather than seeking a common ground of compromise, they staked out their positions and became both rigid and defiant, threatening the health of the entire congregation in the process. Since they were prominent church leaders, it is likely that other members of the church began to take sides. A rift was forming. So Paul wrote to the leaders of the church and said, "I plead with Euodia and I plead with Syntyche to agree with each other in the Lord. Yes, and I ask you, loyal friends, [to] help these women who have contended at my side in the cause of the gospel."

In Paul's mind, no personal agenda was sufficiently important that it be allowed to jeopardize the health of the whole congregation, which, you remember, he understood to be "the body of Christ." He also advised members of the church to step in as peacemakers, to say a gentle but firm "No" to emerging conflict lest the devil get to take a vacation in Philippi.

One of the beauties of the church I serve is that its people do not let differences become divisive. That is a profoundly faithful witness. And, as much of an oxymoron as this may seem to be, I frequently tell our people, "If there is one thing you have in common, it is how different you are!" They are old and they are young; they are conservative and they are liberal; they are Republicans and they are Democrats; they are African American, Caribbean American, Asian American, Native American, Middle Eastern, and Caucasian; they are straight and they are gay; they represent every social and economic demographic. They also have wide and varied ideas about what churches are meant to be and to do. Some of them are social activists, some are committed to the sacramental and liturgical nature of church, some feel that church should primarily be a hospital for the emotionally hurting, and some believe that it should be an academy where we come regularly to learn the faith and how it relates to our lives in our worlds. Yet, when they come into their church home, they teach us what the words of the old song actually mean: "We are one in the Spirit. We are one in the Lord!" They allow for and regularly affirm each person's unique and individual understanding of the nature of church and his or her contribution to that specific purpose. And so I frequently implore them, "Don't ever change because this world needs your witness."

How many times have we heard stories of congregations that rarely argue about feeding the hungry, housing the homeless, battling prejudice and discrimination, creating inclusivity, building programs for church growth, etc., but instead become embroiled in passionate controversies about landscaping, who gets a place in the church cemetery, or what color carpet should be installed in the parlor? I am personally aware of a situation a number of years ago in which a congregation needed to build a new sanctuary. There was no disagreement about that, as the old sanctuary was too small and required constant upkeep. An architect was hired, plans were drawn, and the church members quickly approved the project and began to make plans for a capital campaign. However, a group of church leaders felt that the future of the church would be best served if the new sanctuary faced the road to the north of the church property, as it had a greater volume of traffic and thus might attract increased numbers of visitors. Another group desired to keep the new sanctuary facing the road to the south of the property, as had always been the case for that church. Thus, they feared facing north might symbolically imply turning their backs on their history. An argument ensued, eventuating in a split. Today there are two churches within a half-mile of one another, one facing north and the other facing south. Each church struggles financially and in terms of volunteers required to maintain full programming, whereas jointly they could have had a considerable impact on that entire area of the city. This is an astounding story, isn't it, especially for those of us who believe that one of the essentials of being church is unity amid diversity?

Even if congregations manage to keep conflicts to a remarkable minimum, however, as individuals we still sometimes experience conflicts in the world. In the marketplace. In the apartment complex. In the family unit. We know what it's like in interpersonal ways for one to face north and the other to face south. We have our Euodia and Syntyche moments. So how do we cope with those experiences? What lessons from Paul's advice to the Philippian church might be applied to our lives when conflicts arise?

Paul wrote, "Let your gentleness be known to all . . . and the peace of God which passes all understanding will guard your hearts and minds in Christ Jesus."

Gentleness is not always the standard we apply toward others with whom we have disagreements, despite the fact that Jesus encouraged us to treat others as we'd like to be treated. When arguments and conflicts arise, too often gentleness falls out of the equation like Eutychus from an upstairs window (Acts 20:9). Why does that happen?

A frequent reason is that we are often convinced of our own position about a particular issue without adequately considering or carefully listening to the position of someone else. Maxwell Perkins, the editor, wrote, "One of my deepest convictions is that the terrible harms that are done in this world are not done by deliberately evil people. . . . They are done by basically good people who are so sure that God is with them. Nothing can stop them, for they are certain that they are right."[13] Years ago I heard the brilliant Christian ethicist, the late Dr. George Kelsey, make a similar remark in a lecture at Drew University. He said, "Some of the most heinous acts ever committed were done by people who thought that God was on their side." "Heinous" is a conservative description of acts committed in the murders of children in a school in Pakistan, journalists in a publishing building in France, and hundreds of innocent victims of Boko Haram in Nigeria. But each time, the murderers who committed those unthinkable acts of cruelty claimed to do so in defense of God.

There is little doubt that Euodia and Syntyche were good people who believed in God, but each apparently also believed that God was on her side and therefore staked herself out in adversarial fashion out on a particular issue. Good people, we understand, are just as likely as anyone else to be more influenced by ego than by faith, seized (if only momentarily) by the need to be right. So Paul wrote and reminded them of how godliness shows through in a person's life. It reveals itself not by making authoritarian decisions that "God is on my side" but rather, he said, by letting "your gentleness be known by all." At the outset of what may become a full-blown conflict, what could possibly be lost by at least listening to and carefully considering the idea of the other person? Many a heated argument or ruptured friendship could be avoided by a simple decision: "Let's talk about this together. I'm not sure either of us fully understands what the other is saying, and our relationship matters enough to make sure that we hear one another."

Paul also referred to *the peace that passes understanding.* Frequently we clergy use that phrase to describe the spirit of comfort our faith brings to us in moments of stress or sadness. And whereas that is theologically true, in this particular biblical lesson it is not exegetically accurate. In this passage, Paul is literally talking about becoming peacemakers when doing so seems illogical. He is talking about taking specific actions to reduce conflict and establish communications and concord. This requires some self-analysis regarding one's unique situation:

• Will I create an environment for listening?
• Am I open to employing a relational methodology that includes each party's stating what it "thinks" the other party's position is, allowing for explanation and clarification if and where perceptions are inaccurate?
• Do I need a third person to mediate?
• Will I make my responses face-to-face (or at least voice-to-voice) instead of by text or e-mail?
• Am I willing to establish mutually acceptable ground rules for shared behavior while discussing an interpersonal conflict?
• If the other person agrees, will I begin and close the conversation (or each conversation) with shared prayer?

• Will I proceed always with the teachings of Jesus in mind, remembering his words, "Do unto others as you would have them do unto you"?

Paul called Euodia and Syntyche to rise above the limitations of self and to love another person who made loving difficult. When we do that (when we take concrete and often difficult actions to defuse conflict and create concord), we help create a "peace that passes all understanding."

Of course, the temptation sneaks in to think, "Hey, I am only human. I have feet of clay. My feelings get hurt, and I sometimes become reactive rather than proactive." How do we overcome that in order to deal lovingly and peacefully with other people? Paul suggested an answer that has to do with our *mindset*. "Whatever is true," he wrote, "whatever is noble, whatever is right, whatever is pure, whatever is lovely, whatever is admirable . . . think about those things."

He told Euodia and Syntyche and any who were tempted to join forces with them to refocus. Focus your thoughts on the Spirit, the goodness, and the beauties of God. Try to see the world through Christ's eyes. Abandon the old win/lose way of looking at life. In Christian relations, he wrote, the priority is not to get in one's own way.

In a world of anger, recrimination, prejudice, abuse, "wars and rumors of wars," I found it sobering and inspiring some time ago to hear a former astronaut reflect in a TV interview about his journey into space. Speaking of how it looked to peer down on the shining blue orb that is Earth, he said, "When you see it from that perspective, you realize it is one small neighborhood in a vast Universe. We who live upon the planet are all neighbors with one another. And thus war and hatred become unthinkable, since we are all called to keep the neighborhood clean and peaceful."

So it is with planet Earth. So it is with Christian congregations. And so it is with interpersonal relationships. Thus, Paul told the people in Philippi that discord and hatred were unthinkable in their shared neighborhood of faith. You and I, as members of "the Body of Christ," are asked to keep the neighborhood clean and peaceful, to show the world what love, grace, and compassion look like. In order to do so, we focus our attention on that which is "noble, pure, lovely, and admirable." As Paul said, "Think on those things," and we will be empowered to become peacemakers.

Reflection

1. What things should my church do to promote peace rather than disunity? How may I personally make that happen as a church member?

_____

_____

_____

_____

2. Discuss or consider the role of ego in most conflict situations (whether in churches, government, businesses, or interpersonal relationships).

_____

_____

_____

_____

3. When a conflict exists, what are some specific, practical methods for resolving it? Describe what you understand to be honest but compassionate conversation.

_____

_____

_____

_____

Clichés Worth Considering

The proverbs of Solomon, son of David, king of Israel: That all may know wisdom and instruction, understand words of insight, receive instruction in wise dealing, righteousness, justice, and equity; that prudence may be given to the simple, knowledge and discretion to the youth—the wise also may hear and increase in learning, and those of understanding acquire skill, to understand a proverb and a figure, the words of the wise and their riddles. The knowledge of the LORD is the beginning of wisdom. (Proverbs 1:1-7)

Often we hear someone dismiss a piece of advice by saying, "That is so clichéd." We all know what that means. A cliché is a proverb, a wisdom statement so timeworn and familiar that often we ignore it as being outdated or worthless. But I have always believed that ordinarily clichés become clichés because time has consistently proven them to be true. Think of a few you heard from your grandparents, which they probably heard from theirs:

- "It's better to light a single candle than to curse the darkness."
- "A fool and his money are soon parted."
- "A leopard doesn't change its spots."
- "People who live in glass houses shouldn't throw stones."
- "Laugh, and the world laughs with you."

Those adages became clichés because time proved them to be true . . . to be words of wisdom that, for the most part, we could count on.

The book of Proverbs is part of a collection of biblical writings called "Wisdom Literature." The verses at the beginning of this chapter appear in a passage that concludes with the statement that is also translated, "the respect of the LORD is the beginning of wisdom." The passage begins (in fact, the book of Proverbs begins) with a statement of its purpose is: that "all may know wisdom and understand words of insight and receive instruction" on how best to find life worth living. Then the book proceeds with a rapid-fire succession of proverbs (usually brief, concise wisdom statements), more or less clichés that became such because time proved them to be true.

So, far from dismissing clichés, our faith says we should listen, discern, take them seriously, and learn from them so that we "may know wisdom and understand words of insight and receive instruction" on how best to find a life worth living. And these wisdom statements apply equally whether our topic is an individual life journey or the life and witness of a particular congregation.

Let me share a few of my favorite clichés, things we have heard so often across the years that now we almost listen without hearing, without actually paying attention. I think they deserve to be heard, as if for the first time, because they are bearers of Truth.

How about this one? *A picture is worth a thousand words.* That's true, of course.

I was browsing through a local bookstore recently and came across the biography of Robert Ripley. What a fascinating man. He was bullied as a child, particularly because of his looks. He lost his first job as a newspaper journalist because the editor thought his work was not up to standards. But in time he proved his early critics wrong. He found himself, and what a creative and curious legacy he left behind. My younger son, Zachary, and I walked through Ripley's Believe It Or Not Museum on 42nd Street some time ago. It's impossible not to be utterly intrigued when you do so, as you observe photos and artifacts from Robert Ripley's global travels in the last century. It is likewise impossible not to be utterly intrigued when you read his biography—all about his boyhood, his failures and successes as a journalist, his less-than-perfect marriage, and his career as a cartoonist, an entrepreneur, a world traveler, a radio personality, a friend of the stars, and ultimately a collector of unbelievable things and stories that would become his lasting legacy. It was an interesting read. But do you know what was even more interesting and what underscored the story of his life in ways that words on a page could not do? It was the countless photos contained in the book—photos of Ripley on every continent, standing alongside people of unusual statures, holding in his hands shrunken heads and buried treasures, uncovering things that, had he not found them, would have seemed like fiction, maybe even like science fiction. His life's story took on depth and dimension when you were able to see it with your own eyes.

So it is, I think, with faith. We read about people of faith. We hear their stories. This increases our beliefs and empowers our spirits. And yet the most powerful impact of faith that any of us ever experiences is seeing faith lived out by another person or a gathering of the faithful (a local congregation). We witness their acts of kindness or sacrifice, their deeds of mercy or reconciliation, their shining faces of joy, their bowed heads of prayer, and what we observe in them changes us. Isn't that what the author of the epistle of James was getting at when he said, "I by my works will show you my faith" (2:18)? A picture is worth a thousand words. So, no matter how much you or I may talk about God or Jesus or love, what makes a lasting difference is when others see the love of God in us and feel it through us. If they watch you and me individually, and our churches corporately, offer gifts of charity or express words of encouragement or perform deeds of love, if they actually can witness that in us, what they see will change their lives.

How about this cliché? *Money can't buy happiness.* Phyllis Diller once quoted that statement and added, "Maybe not, but it can make misery a lot easier to deal with!" I understand that, of course. There is nothing wrong or sinful with being materially rich. Think of the philanthropists who have used their resources in education, medical research, and a host of other ways that make life better for everyone. Think of the congregations that have made transforming impacts in whole communities because they used their money as tools to enhance lives. Do not misinterpret this as a condemnation of those who have resources. Most of us, myself included, wish that we had more. The point is, however, that having more does not ultimately bring peace or meaning or joy to life.

One of the richest men of the twentieth century, an industrial tycoon worth billions of dollars years ago when money went so much further than it does now, said on his deathbed, "How late I learned that what I needed most was friends." He was surrounded by opulence but faced the end without love. Steve Jobs was correct in reminding us that "success does not mean being the wealthiest man in the cemetery."

Happiness (better put, a sense of being satisfied with life) is not dependent on possessions but instead on purpose. It's not what we take that brings meaning. It is, instead, what we give. Do we make life better for people? Do we make them happier somehow . . . or safer . . . or more hopeful or encouraged? Do we strengthen their sense of faith? Do we make them feel valued? Do we keep anyone from going to bed hungry? Do we help protect any vulnerable person who has suffered abuse? When people speak of us behind our backs, are they able to say the same things they would say to our faces? Do they speak of us with appreciation and affection because of what they see in us or feel from us? Or do they say of us individually, "That guy is all about himself," or congregationally, "They've never figured out the difference between being a church and being a bank"? The things (endeavors, commitments, characteristics) that bring satisfaction to life are, indeed, things that money cannot buy. Maybe that's part of what Jesus intended to articulate when he said, "Share what you have with the poor, and you will have treasure in heaven" (Matt 19:21).

How about one more cliché worth considering? Obviously, I could mention a hundred, but I will trust you to do that on your own (to reconsider clichés that perhaps you have too easily dismissed and from which you might find meaning or Truth). For now, let's look at just one more.

President Franklin Delano Roosevelt made this statement famous: *the only thing we have to fear is fear itself.* William Barclay used to say that worry, or excessive fear, is essentially distrust of God. By that he was not critiquing people who are wise or cautious in the face of danger. He was commenting about people who are paralyzed in the face of life.

I will always look before crossing the street. I will always avoid poison, rattlesnakes, and rabid dogs. I will always seek shelter if I witness approaching tornadoes or nearby lightning. I will never play Russian roulette. I have a healthy fear of heights and thus will never test that fear by skydiving or bungee jumping. There is a difference between caution and terror, between being smart about threatening things and being immobilized by the inherent risks of life.

Some people, however, do the latter. They are afraid to step out of comfort zones, to try new things, to meet new people, to chase new dreams. I know a relatively young man with good relational skills and a capable intellect. And yet he is a consistent underachiever, remaining within the safety of a go-nowhere kind of job and stuck in a romance with a person who expects even less from life than he does. Some time ago he told me of the dreams he harbors deep inside, dreams for a better life, a brighter future, a more significant outlet for his creative side. I simply asked, "If you have the dreams, why don't you pursue them?" He answered with a poignant note of resignation, "I have never succeeded at anything yet. I just don't want to fail anymore." His past now dictates the limits that are placed on his future (not limits that God placed, for God has given him a plethora of talents, but limits that fear has placed). He is so afraid of failing that he refuses to try, and in refusing to try, he condemns himself to ongoing failure. The cycle is easy to see. Fear motivates him and thus restricts him.

If, however, he allowed faith to be his motivation (faith in God and in himself), then those locked doors of restriction would be thrown open, and the dreams he feels but dares not chase might become his reality.

Wouldn't you hate to be ninety years old, sitting in a rocking chair at a retirement home, looking back across your life and thinking, "If only . . . ." "If only I had tried." "If only I had possessed the nerve, the courage, the self-confidence, the faith." "If only I had known then what I know now." When we allow fear to be the dominant force in our lives, that is the sort of future fear will construct for us.

Again, this principle holds true with local churches. Though every congregation should be wise and discerning in making choices, sometimes our motivation is based more on the fear factor than the faith factor, resulting in eventual, and sometimes regretful, assessment of the choices we did not make. Why did a congregation choose not to initiate a new mission program, to begin work on a new facility addition, to establish a new worship service, or to employ a new staff person for children or youth ministries? Was it from fear that doing such may stretch them unnecessarily from a financial standpoint, and thus they waited? Rarely does a church say "No." Ordinarily, the response is "Not yet." "We can't afford it now, but the time will come." And the time does come, but often it comes for the congregation down the street or around the block that had a sense of courage to match its sense of vision.

We often hear what we have heard before and dismissively we say, "Oh, that is such a cliché." We quit listening when, in fact, it became a cliché because it is true. And thus it has a powerful Truth to share with us, if we would listen, a Truth that could perhaps transform our lives. The author of Proverbs understood that, so he quoted adages that may have already been clichés when he wrote them down. Certainly now, three millennia later, they are. And they have stuck around so long because time has proved them worthy. So here's my advice. Read the book of Proverbs, and see what some of those old teachings say to our modern world. Think of some clichés you heard from your parents or grandparents, and listen to them as if you were hearing them for the first time. Let Truth find you, even in what is so familiar that we almost tune it out. For, as Proverbs reminds us, it is God's will that "all may know wisdom and understand words of insight and receive instruction" on how best to find life worth living.

Reflection

1. Discuss or consider the meaning of the advice St. Francis gave to the Friars as he sent them out: "Share the gospel, and use words if you must."

_____

_____

_____

_____

2. What is the appropriate role of money in the life of discipleship?

_____

_____

_____

_____

3. What might your church accomplish if it were more intentionally and consistently motivated by faith instead of fear?

_____

_____

_____

_____

An I-Centered Church

Now the eleven disciples went to Galilee, to the mountain to which Jesus had directed them. And when they saw him they worshiped him; but some doubted. And Jesus came and said to them, "All authority in heaven and on earth has been given to me. Go therefore and make disciples of all nations, baptizing them in the name of the Father and of the Son and of the Holy Spirit, teaching them to observe all that I have commanded you; and lo, I am with you always, to the close of the age." (Matthew 28:16-20)

For if I preach the gospel, that gives me no ground for boasting. For necessity is laid upon me. Woe to me if I do not preach the gospel! For if I do this of my own will, I have a reward; but if not of my own will, I am entrusted with a commission. What then is my reward? Just this: that in my preaching I may make the gospel free of charge, not making full use of my right in the gospel. For though I am free from all, I have made myself a slave to all, that I might win the more. To the Jews I became as a Jew, in order to win Jews; to those under the law I became as one under the law—though not being myself under the law—that I might win those under the law. To those outside the law I became as one outside the law—not being without law toward God but under the law of Christ—that I might win those outside the law. To the weak I became weak, that I might win the weak. I have become all things to all people, that I might by all means save some. I do it all for the sake of the gospel, that I may share in its blessings. (1 Corinthians 9:16-23)

A little boy was told to say his bedtime prayers, while his parents stood by and watched. They were filled with pride when he reverently knelt beside his bed, bowed his head, and folded his hands. But the sweet ambiance ended when they heard him say:

God take care of me and my friends.
Just see that we are blest.

And once You've taken care of us,
The devil can have the rest."

To lift up the importance of being an I-centered church sounds about as small and self-absorbed as that child's prayer. However, in this case the phrase is simply a literary device to address what the Great Commission calls churches to be and to do.

In a meeting of a church-visioning committee, people began to suggest words they felt described a variety of activities that should be at the center of what "church" means. I quickly located a mustard-stained napkin in my coat pocket and began to write their words down. The four on which we focused that night, oddly enough, all started with the letter "I." It was there that I began to understand some of the biblical beauty of being an I-centered church.

The first word was *Invite*. It turned out to be a singularly important word because we decided that night to make it one of the three operative ideas for the next several years in the life of our congregation. Those involved in the decision felt that any church worthy of the title *Christian* is by definition called to be warm, welcoming, hospitable, and invitational.

Imagine yourself in the military, boarding a plane to some faraway land where we still have peacekeeping forces. You are aware that you do, indeed, stand in harm's way. You are aware, therefore, that the possibility exists that you will not make a return trip home. Imagine your spouse and children standing close by in tears, saying a good-bye that they do not want to say. You wonder if you'll ever see them again in this world. In that moment, what would you say to people whom you love more than life itself? My guess is you would not waste the final moment before boarding the plane talking about sports, weather, fashion, or re-roofing the house. Rather, you would tell your family that you love them, that you will be praying for them and hope they will be praying for you. You would want your final words to be the most important words possible to speak to those you love.

When Jesus was about to ascend into heaven, he stood for the final time with his disciples—the people whom he loved like family. He had to determine the one last word he wished to share with them, the one final message he hoped they would not forget. And what did he say? "Go into all the world, making disciples." The final word, the lasting message, of the Messiah had to do with invitation, welcome, inclusivity, and hospitality, with reaching out beyond the walls of the church and bringing others in. If it were that important to Jesus, how could it be anything less than crucial to us?

Sixty percent of Americans are functionally un-churched. Half of those people say they do not attend because no one has ever invited them to any church at any time. That is an amazing statistic if, in fact, we take seriously the final words of Jesus.

The second word I wrote down that night was *Involve*. As noted in considering the word *Invite*, there is a place at God's table for everyone. Everyone. In Paul's letter to the Corinthians, he spoke of a church of "slaves and free," "Jews and Gentiles," "those who live by the Law and those who are weak." In short, Paul was telling the church in Corinth that all people are valued and wanted. It is equally true that all people are likewise needed. All have something of worth to give, and the church needs their unique gifts.

When you enter a church, you bring skills, talents, and dreams with you. And there is room for the unique gifts you bring. Simply sitting in a sanctuary for one hour a week makes you part of a congregation. But when you become part of a small group, a Bible study class, a choir, an action committee, a task force that is service-oriented, the ushers, a youth orga-nization, a mission trip fellowship, a drama group, a softball team, or any of a hundred different circles of like-minded congregants, then you have become part of the fellowship. When you bring your talents to a specific area of the life of the church, the church becomes stronger and you no longer feel like a stranger there. Instead, you are part of the family.

Studies by religious sociologists from Miller to Schaller to Barna and a host of others consistently reveal the same conclusion. Survey after survey, study after study, indicates that people desire to be part of a congregation where they can put their faith into practice, where they can live out their discipleship. Surveys done among people who have made recent decisions to join a particular church indicate that they visited because they were invited, but the majority joined because they were assured of an opportu-nity to become involved in doing something to make the community or the world a better place.

A third word we discussed that night was *Instruct*. In the Great Commission, Jesus told the disciples to "Go into all the world making disciples, baptizing them in the name of the Father, the Son, and the Holy Spirit, and teaching them . . . ."

A friend of mine who is a minister told me of a man in his congrega-tion who was faithful in church attendance. He attended worship services, church suppers, and all manner of special events. However, he never attended study classes and educational events. No matter how often his friends in the church might invite him, he always refused to be present for those occasions. This is what he would say in declining their invitations: "I already know more than I'm willing to do!"

Jesus would have taken issue with that. So should we. As parents, spouses, partners, professionals, or Christians, we never know enough. When I was in seminary, it seemed odd to me to notice how many retired professors made daily pilgrimages to the library. There you would find them in the stacks, bending over old theological volumes, taking notes as if they were students or were still preparing to teach. In those long-ago days, I wondered why anyone would choose to do that if they didn't have to. Now I wonder why anyone would ever stop doing it. It is the journey of the mind that keeps us young. God has countless undiscovered treasures for those who continue to seek.

Among the most important things we do in church are any activities that strengthen our sense of an academy presence (Sunday school classes, Vacation Bible School, small group Bible studies, theological exploration groups, lectures or book studies, or any forums where we open ourselves to God's wisdom). The journey toward knowledge, especially spiritual knowledge, makes life exciting and keeps our spirits vibrant and vital.

The final word discussed that night was *Inspire*. Paul was the poster boy of what it means to be inspired. He was virtually "on fire" to be about God's business. He wrote, "I am compelled to preach. Woe unto me if I preach not the gospel!" (1 Cor 9:16). He had a story to share, and he would not rest until he shared it.

An Army private was assigned to a base in Kansas. His girlfriend lived in Oklahoma. Every Friday he would ask for a weekend pass in order to go visit her. And every week the commanding officer would give the pass to someone else. Finally, after everyone in his barracks had been given a weekend of freedom, the private knew that it had to be his turn at last. Instead, to his absolute surprise, the C.O. bypassed him and gave the weekend's privileges to someone who had previously been awarded a pass. This straw broke the camel's back. That night, the disappointed soldier hopped into a Jeep and drove toward the main gate. The guard on duty shouted, "Halt!" but the young private kept coming. The guard leveled his rifle at the Jeep and once more shouted, "Halt!" This time the driver yelled back, "I have a mama in heaven, a daddy in hell, and a girlfriend in Oklahoma.

And I plan to see one of them tonight!" He was a man on a mission. He was inspired.

As people of faith, it is reasonable to think that we should always be inspired. We Christians have the greatest message on earth to share. We have been given a secret that can end hostility between individuals and nations, that can bring confidence to those who are afraid, hope to those who are discouraged, peace to those who are troubled, and love to those who feel unspeakably alone. Believers know what a difference the Prince of Peace can make in a human life. And that should inspire us, sometimes with words of faith and other times with deeds of courage or kindness, to share the good news with others. How can we experience Jesus' power, comfort, and love but refuse to pass it along to others who struggle and suffer? As Paul said, "I am compelled to preach. Woe unto me if I preach not the gospel!"

In that church-visioning committee meeting, I eavesdropped on some of the finest and most faithful Christians I know. As they talked, I jotted down on a napkin their vision of an I-centered church. It is a vision of a church that Invites, Involves, Instructs, and Inspires. That is precisely what Jesus had in mind when he said, "Go into all the world, making disciples of all people, baptizing them in the name of the Father, and of the Son, and of the Holy Spirit, and teaching them. . . . Lo! I will be with you, always."

Reflection

1. What things could my church do to attract more first-time visitors?

_____

_____

_____

_____

2. How can a church effectively help its members employ their individual gifts and graces for ministry?

_____

_____

_____

_____

3. Discuss or consider the role of Christian education in the overall life of a church. What can a church do to challenge the minds of individuals? How can a church develop an "academy presence" in a community? How can a church partner with institutions of higher education in order to offer a stronger ministry to the congregation and to the community at large?

_____

_____

_____

_____

A Praiseworthy Church

To all the saints in Christ Jesus who are at Philippi, with the bishops and deacons: Grace to you and peace from God our Father and the Lord Jesus Christ. I thank my God in all my remembrance of you, always in every prayer of mine for you all, making my prayer with joy, thankful for your partnership in the gospel from the first day until now. And I am sure that he who began a good work in you will bring it to completion at the day of Jesus Christ. (Philippians 1:1-6)

. . . . [I]t was kind of you to share my trouble. And you Philippians yourselves know that in the beginning of the gospel, when I left Macedonia, no church entered into partnership with me in giving and receiving except you only; for even in Thessalonica you sent me help once and again. And my God will supply every need of yours according to his riches in glory in Christ Jesus. To our God and Father be glory for ever and ever. Amen. (Philippians 4:14-16, 19)

And he came also to Derbe and to Lystra. A disciple was there, named Timothy, the son of a Jewish woman who was a believer; but his father was a Greek. He was well spoken of by the brethren at Lystra and Iconium. Paul wanted Timothy to accompany him; and he took him and circumcised him because of the Jews that were in those places, for they all knew that his father was a Greek. As they went on their way through the cities, they delivered to them for observance the decisions which had been reached by the apostles and elders who were at Jerusalem. So the churches were strengthened in the faith, and they increased in numbers daily.

. . . . [A] vision appeared to Paul in the night: a man of Macedonia was standing beseeching him and saying, "Come over to Macedonia and help us." And when he had seen the vision, immediately we sought

to go on into Macedonia, concluding that God had called us to preach the gospel to them.

Setting sail therefore from Troas, we made a direct voyage to Samothrace, and the following day to Neapolis, and from there to Philippi, which is the leading city of the district of Macedonia, and a Roman colony. We remained in this city some days; and on the sabbath day we went outside the gate to the riverside, where we supposed there was a place of prayer; and we sat down and spoke to the women who had come together. One who heard us was a woman named Lydia, from the city of Thyatira, a seller of purple goods, who was a worshiper of God. The Lord opened her heart to give heed to what was said by Paul. And when she was baptized, with her household, she besought us, saying, "If you have judged me to be faithful to the Lord, come to my house and stay." And she prevailed upon us. (Acts 16:9-15)

A woman stepped into the confessional booth at her local Roman Catholic church. Peeking through the shutters, she saw the face of a man she did not know. "Pardon me," she said, "but you are not Father O'Flannery. Are you a new priest I haven't met yet?"

The man answered, "No ma'am. I'm just in here to polish the woodwork."

"Well," the woman continued, "where is Father O'Flannery?"

The custodian whispered, "I'm not sure, lady. But judging from what some of his church members have said to me since I sat down in this box, I hope he's gone to get the police!"

Every church has its own collection of people who would've brought a sense of surprise to the custodian in the confessional box. Some of those people are in the pews; others are in the pulpits. We just don't always confess it. But, as Paul said, "All have sinned and fall short of the glory of God."

A fable is told about what happened when God created animals to put on the earth. A group of angels saw God at work and said, "That looks like fun." So God allowed them to get together as a committee and told them they could create one new animal. The angels could not agree on what kind of animal to create. Some liked one type, some another. Eventually they compromised and created the platypus—an animal with a bill of a duck, the fur of an otter, the tale of the beaver, and the feet of a frog. Subsequently, God decreed that there would be no more committees in heaven! Churches not only have sinners; they also have committees, which in some circumstances can be even worse.

It is easy to find fault with congregations, if that is what we are predisposed to do: faulting them for what they fail to do, for what they choose to do, for how they choose to do it. That is not a new thing. Read Colossians, Ephesians, Corinthians, the description of the seven churches in Revelation, or almost any of the New Testament epistles. In those letters you will read of churches that tried the patience of the saints.

But there is one that is different, almost pure in its Christlikeness, a model of what a church is designed to be. Again, as previously noted, that church was the one in Philippi. It remains the New Testament's model of what true churches are meant to be (in spite of the rare cases of people like Euodia and Syntheche whom we considered earlier). When Paul wrote to the Philippian church, he said, "I thank God in all my remembrance of you." That is an extraordinary statement. In spite of those who may have been broken or misguided, in spite of committees, in spite of human faults and frailties, there was something about the congregation in Philippi that made Paul pray a prayer of thanks every time he thought of them.

Paul, literally in love with the Philippian church, wrote, "For God is my witness, how I yearn for you all with the affection of Jesus Christ" (Phil 1:8).

One of the things Paul appreciated most was that *the Philippians loved him in his times of loneliness and despair.* He referred to "Epaphroditus . . . your messenger and minister to my needs" (Phil 2:25). While he was in a Roman prison, doubtless feeling alone and afraid, the people in Philippi did not settle for sending him Christmas cards or fruit baskets. They sent a man named Epaphroditus to stay there, to be with Paul in his suffering, to make sure he was being treated fairly and was healthy, and to remind him that he had not been forgotten.

A woman whose husband committed suicide told me her story. After it happened, she was understandably devastated, as were their children. But she reported that every week a woman from their church visited. "Sometimes," she said, "she would sit and listen to me. Sometimes she would help me with thank-you notes. Sometimes she would straighten the kitchen. Sometimes she would help my children with their homework. And sometimes she would just put her arm around my shoulders while I cried. But every time she came, I knew my church was there and my God was there. Somehow, I think because of that I survived."

Paul praised the Philippian church because it reached out to him in his dark and desperate moments, wrapping an arm around his shoulders. That is what Christlike churches do. He commended them for sending "Epaph-roditus . . . your messenger and minister to my needs."

Another reason Paul loved the church in Philippi was because *it believed in missional ministry.* Here's how he put it: "Even in Thessalonica you sent me help once and again" (Phil 4:16). Throughout his ministry, Paul labored to raise funds for the needy, especially for the young Christians in Jerusalem who were facing persecution and financial disaster. Unfortunately, not all the churches he established were overtly generous. But Philippi was. Many scholars believe that most of the church people in Philippi were not partic-ularly wealthy. Even so, they set aside money from their sometimes paltry incomes to help others who had even less.

A devoted disciple of Christ named Dr. Joe Hale for many years led the World Methodist Council, circling the globe countless times in that capacity. He preached in the great shrines and cathedrals of the world. He also walked through jungles to share the good news in the open air or beneath straw arbors. He probably understood more about the unique role of the church on every continent than anyone I ever knew. I heard Dr. Hale say in a sermon many years ago that churches survive and grow primarily because they do not stop with preaching; they also practice. He said that every time you find tragedy or need in this world, there you also find church people devotedly trying to heal the hurts. Fill in the denom-inational blank—Lutheran, UMC, AME, CME, Presbyterian, Baptist, Roman Catholic, Episcopal, RCA, etc. The story is always the same. Chris-tian churches do not stop with preaching; they also practice. One of the most inspiring witnesses in recent memory in our area is what happened in the wake of Hurricane Sandy. Churches of all denominations across America sent tens of millions of dollars and countless volunteers to help in rebuilding efforts and to heal folks whom they would never meet or know. More than preaching, people of faith practiced what they profess to believe, and we were the beneficiaries.

The people in Philippi never missed a chance to reach out to others in an effort to heal hurts. They were diligent in helping those who could not help themselves. And that, as much as anything else, led Paul to say, "I thank God in all my remembrance of you."

There is a third thing: *the Philippian church was evangelistic and inclusive.* Everyone was welcome there, and everyone was wanted. Acts 16 describes the make-up of the Philippian church. It mentions a woman named Lydia, a wealthy Asian merchant in whose house the congregation often met. It also mentions a jailer, a middle-class citizen of Rome who lived and worked in Philippi. And then it mentions a local slave woman who was an impoverished fortune teller, and, until Paul got there, literally owned by some of the men in Philippi. A rich foreign businesswoman, a middle-class working Roman government official, and a local slave girl who was at the bottom of society's totem pole—and they were all welcome, all wanted, and all of equal importance in the Philippian church. It was a church with open doors, open arms, and open hearts. It was a church that reached out with passion to invite others in, and loved them once they got there.

That is one of the things I admire so deeply and dearly about the church I serve. We look the way the world looks. There is room for all here. No one is left out or left behind. Color doesn't matter. Age doesn't matter. Gender doesn't matter. Orientation doesn't matter. Economics don't matter. Politics don't matter. How you look or where you live or what you drive don't matter. What matters is that we are all part of one family and all children of the same God.

When my friend Bill Quick was assigned to a large church in downtown Detroit, he discovered a great, impressive, historic building that was slowly becoming an empty showplace to the distant past, when leading Detroit aristocracy had kept the church alive and bursting at the seams. Over the years, the environment around the church campus had changed. Most of the wealthy had moved away. Suburbs were now the centers of growth and commerce. The area surrounding the church was in economic decline. People felt unsafe coming out for night meetings, as you could look through the windows on one side of the building and see prostitutes and circling cars. You could look out the other side and see drug deals going down. All the "nice folks" who loved their church and continued to drive in from the suburbs to worship there did so in spite of personal fears. But then that newly arrived preacher said to his people, "We have two choices. We can build bigger fences and hide from our parish, or we can open our doors and evangelize it."

To their everlasting credit, the people at that Detroit congregation chose option two. They went out into the surrounding neighborhoods, out into the streets, and said to the people they found there, "We want you to be with us." In time, the old-establishment types who had remained began to say, "Our church is a rainbow." All colors, classes, and backgrounds were wanted and welcomed there. Friends who know what is going on at ground level tell me that the church is more alive now than it has ever been. There's a sanctuary full of people of all colors; people in tailored clothes share hymnals with people who have hardly anything to wear, nurses sit next to sex-workers, businessmen next to street people, mansions owners co-chair committees with people from the projects. An old church in need of reviving has been resurrected because they opened their doors and hearts and invited people on the outside to come in.

There are myriad lessons to be learned from churches like that. Perhaps the primary lesson is that we all know people on the outside who need to be invited in. It will make them better and stronger if they come. And it will make our congregations better and stronger, too. Every active churchgoer knows an average of seven people who are not actively involved in church, four of whom would come next Sunday if we simply invited them. There's an important key to building a healthy future for your congregation. People need the church. Likewise, every church needs people. If we love our church, and if we love people, and if we love Christ, then not a week should pass when we do not invite someone to come and worship with us.

The Philippians, probably more than any other New Testament congregation, were a praiseworthy church. They modeled what real churches ought to be. And the secret was simple.

In the name of Christ, they loved lonely or frightened people. They helped needy or hurting people. And they invited and welcomed all people.

Because of that, Paul said, "I thank God in all my remembrance of you."

Reflection

1. Discuss or consider how a variety of social, economic, cultural, and ethnic groups add to the life of any Christian community of believers.

_____

_____

_____

_____

2. What basic discipleship commitments should my congregation reasonably make? How can I individually assist in honoring and achieving those commitments?

_____

_____

_____

_____

3. Write a mission statement for (a) your personal life as a Christian, and (b) the corporate life of your congregation.

_____

_____

_____

_____

Section Five

Living Faithfully

Scripture is filled with stories of people who were asked to put feet on their faith (as our kids say, not merely to "talk the talk" but to "walk the walk"). From Moses who was urged to lead the Hebrews out of Egypt to Saul who was called to become the first king of Israel, from Esther who was asked to run a potentially life-threatening personal risk to protect her people to David who was asked to do the same by facing a giant, from Peter, Andrew, James, and John who were invited to leave their boats and become fishers of people to Paul whose whole life was redirected while traveling the road to Damascus, with countless similar stories added on, our corpus of faith consistently teaches that at some point the question is not merely "What do you believe?" but instead "What do you do because you believe?"

Discipleship is the word we use to describe the act of responding to one's faith by living faithfully. James, the author of the New Testament epistle and thought by some to be a brother of Jesus, wrote, "Show me your faith apart from your works, and I by my works will show you my faith." He also stated his thesis with even more vigor: "Faith without works is dead" (Jas 2:17-18). Though sometimes accused of being a salvation-by-works text, James makes clear that faith precedes discipleship. But because we believe, as a result of our faith we live in new and different and more specifically helpful ways in the world. We move from talking the talk to walking the walk.

As one approaches the finish line in life and looks back over the course that has been run, which is the more likely (and more meaningful) question: "Did I constantly maintain a defensible theology?" or "Did my life make a difference?" Whereas Christians desire—and need—to live with biblical and theological integrity, at some point that theology, in Jesus' own words, should "bear fruit." What we do in, with, and through our lives matters.

And so we come to the concluding section of the book, simply put: a consideration of what I do because of what I believe (that is, because of Whose I am). Let's consider that together.

World Changers

"Now therefore fear the LORD, *and serve him in sincerity and in faithfulness; put away the gods which your fathers served beyond the River, and in Egypt, and serve the* LORD. *And if you be unwilling to serve the* LORD, *choose this day whom you will serve, whether the gods your fathers served in the region beyond the River, or the gods of the Amorites in whose land you dwell; but as for me and my house, we will serve the* LORD.*" (Joshua 24:14-15)*

Some time ago while standing in the checkout line at our neighborhood D'Agostino's Grocery Store, I was following my regular custom of reading the headlines on the displayed magazines. Oh, the things you can learn in checkout lines: who's dating whom, who's leaving whom, who's having a baby, who just had a face-lift, and what's the latest news about the Kardashians—all the critical data about life's gripping issues.

While reading the covers of several different publications, I spotted a special edition of a nationally popular magazine. The title read "One Hundred People Who Changed the World." On the cover were artists' renderings of people like Martin Luther King, Jr., Gandhi, Mother Teresa, the Beatles, Albert Schweitzer, and on and on. What got my attention, what literally jumped off the cover at me, were two pictures almost side by side of two "world changers," according to that magazine. One was Jesus. The other was Adolph Hitler.

Initially I felt offended even to see their pictures near one another. But then I thought, "Yes. Of course! Each of them did change the world—one for good and the other for evil." And though none of us will ever be as good as Jesus, and I cannot imagine any of us will ever be as evil as Hitler, the choices they made are still the choices you and I have to make. Will we live for good or for evil? Will we be righteous or sinful, kind or cruel, generous or selfish? Will our impact and influence make the world better or worse for those around us? In some sense, you see, we are all world changers. Our challenge is simply to determine what kind of change we want to be.

Remember the words of Gandhi: "We must become the change we wish to see in the world." What kind of world changers do we want to be?

In a famous lesson from Hebrew Scripture, Joshua invites the people on their lengthy pilgrimage to cross the river with him, to finally make their way out of the wilderness into the promised land toward which they have been journeying for such a long, long time. Apparently some of them hesitated. They were not sure they were ready to move forward. So Joshua told them there is no such thing as sitting still in life. We either move ahead or move back. "Choose this day whom you will serve," he told them, even if it were the false gods their ancestors served in Egypt. That would be moving back. He presented to them, of course, a different option, the decision to cross the river and enter the new land of promise. That was the option to move forward. "As for me and my house," said Joshua, "we will serve the LORD." The choice had to be made. There was no such thing as sitting still. Either serve God or serve something else.

And so it is with us. We either serve God or serve something else, but there is no such thing as sitting still. We have to decide whether to be forces of good or forces of evil, people who make life better or make it worse for those around us.

I read an article about marriage in which the author suggested that couples need to "re-up" at seven-year intervals. That is, he wrote that husbands and wives should reassess, decide if they wish to continue, and then negotiate a new contract. In fact, the author said that every marriage should legally conclude every seven years, and that couples would then need to determine whether or not to sign up for another seven. I asked my wife her response to that article. How often did she feel an emotional need to re-up, to re-commit? She said, "That doesn't cross my mind. I made a decision on our wedding day, and I do not have to keep re-deciding." She looked at me for a moment, narrowing her eyes, and then said gently but firmly, "And it better not cross your mind, either." It doesn't.

In much the same sense, somewhere along the line we make a spiritual decision. Either "I am God's" or "I am not." And once we've made the decision, it affects every other decision we make in the future. We do not keep re-deciding. "As for me and my house," said Joshua, "we will serve the LORD." Then they proceeded to cross the river. No looking back. No turning back. They made the decision to serve God, to be influences for good, to make life better for the people of Israel. And so they moved forward.

In like fashion, when our decision to cross the river or to return to Egypt is made, I reiterate: what we decide affects all the other decisions we subsequently make. If I decide to be God's person, then . . .

• I will also decide to be a good listener.
• I will decide to take people seriously.
• I will decide to be patient with others.
• I will decide to help those who are having a difficult time helping themselves.
• I will decide to manage my resources so as to contribute to churches and causes that make a positive difference in the world.
• I will decide to practice kindness (even random acts of kindness) every day.
• I will decide to bite my tongue when tempted to pass along gossip or malevolent criticism.
• I will decide to advocate for people who no longer have sufficient power (such as the very young, the very old, or the very poor).
• I will decide to make a phone call or send an e-mail saying, "Just thinking of you."
• I will decide to laugh more.
• I will decide to love more.

I do not decide every morning whether or not I will live in those ways. Instead, I make a decision to be God's person, to cast my lot for goodness, and that decision sets all the rest into motion.

On the other hand, I am free to decide that God's sort of living demands too much of me. So, as Joshua told the people, I can choose to serve a different god, which inevitably will be the god of self. I will meet my needs. I will exclusively pursue my dreams. I will contribute only to my coffers. I will look out for my best interests. And when I view the world that way, then all others in the world will become merely means to my ends, tools to achieve my desires. The simple truth is, of course, that this sort of living can bring about certain measures of success in terms of power or authority, fame or money. What it will not bring and cannot bring is love. If you love yourself exclusively, no one else would choose to love you. And without love, a person can find everything *except* happiness.

"Choose this day whom you will serve," said Joshua. That will make a profound difference in your world. And it will also make a profound difference in your personal life.

Years ago I visited a woman who was bedridden, near the end of a terminal illness. We talked about her life, which had been as saintly as anyone's I had ever known. She was one of those people who in quiet ways and through small, consistent deeds always made everything and everyone around her better and brighter. That day, she made a statement I have never forgotten. She said, "When I was a young bride, I learned that I was expecting a child. So I made a decision. I decided always to try to live before that child in the way I wanted him or her to live. I would try to make my life an example, a model. I would let my child know what honesty and morals and humor and faith and forgiveness and love look like. So that's how I have tried to live for all my children. [She had three.] I hope it made a difference for them, but this much I know: it has made all the difference for me. Living for good was a good way to live. I've had a truly happy life."

She was correct. Living for good is a good way, in fact, the best way to live, and the inevitable result of that style of living is happiness. Of all the people on the cover of the magazine in the check-out line, the only ones who found lasting joy were those who brought joy to others, those who contributed to the world, those who made a difference for mercy and hope. At some point we all get to decide: Will I be a force for good or evil? In some sense, we are all world changers. Our challenge is simply to determine what kind of change we want to be.

Reflection

1. Describe what you think an "ideal" world, church, and relationship would look like.

_____

_____

_____

_____

2. What steps would have to be taken by global governmental leaders, local congregations, and individuals to help make those dreams come true?

_____

_____

_____

_____

3. In years to come, if your picture appears on the cover of a magazine identifying world changers, what sort of change(s) would you wish to be honored or remembered for?

_____

_____

_____

_____

Relational Needs and Expectations

And Leah conceived and bore a son, and she called his name Reuben; for she said, "Because the Lord has looked upon my affliction; surely now my husband will love me." She conceived again and bore a son, and said, "Because the Lord has heard that I am hated, he has given me this son also"; and she called his name Simeon. Again she conceived and bore a son, and said, "Now this time my husband will be joined to me, because I have borne him three sons"; therefore his name was called Levi. And she conceived again and bore a son, and said, "This time I will praise the Lord"; therefore she called his name Judah; then she ceased bearing. (Genesis 29:32-35)

What if your parents picked out your dates, spouses, or partners for you? In some parts of the world, marriages are still arranged. It was, in fact, a common practice in the days of the Bible. Parents (especially fathers, in that day and age) would make business deals involving their children. If a young man were from a family of prominence and influence, a young woman's parents would try to create a business arrangement whereby it would seem profitable to the boy's parents for him to marry their daughter. By the same token, if a young man's parents assumed that a young woman had a large dowry, then the boy's father would talk to the girl's father in hopes of arranging a marriage fundamentally based on income—but very rarely, in fact almost never, having anything to do with romance or love.

One of the more famous and intriguing stories from Hebrew Scripture tells of the romantic relationships of Jacob and has to do with an arranged marriage. Jacob was working for a man named Laban in the area of Haran. Jacob had met and fallen in love with Laban's younger daughter, Rachel. Apparently she also loved Jacob. So the young man made his intentions known and asked her father for her hand in marriage. But Laban, true to the traditions of that day and age, more or less asked the question, "What's in it for me?" In other words, "What are you offering? What are you bringing to the table that would seal the deal?"

Here was the deal: Jacob would work for Laban for a period of seven years, and then he could marry Rachel. It's a long (and sometimes weird and sometimes steamy) story. It even borders on being incestuous, as Jacob and Rachel were first cousins. However, we cannot read our cultural values back thousands of years into other cultures that operated under different rules. The bottom line is simply that Jacob kept his end of the bargain, put in seven years' work for the woman he loved, and then went to Laban and said, "Now I have honored our covenant, so may I have the hand of your daughter in marriage?" And Laban gave him the hand of his daughter—just not the daughter Jacob was counting on. Rachel had an older sister named Leah, and custom was that a younger daughter could not marry until the older one was wed. During the seven years while Jacob was waiting for Rachel, no one had married Leah. Long story short: Jacob wound up married to Leah and working another seven years in order to finally earn the woman of his dreams, the one he had hoped to marry in the first place.

Okay, let's forget arranged marriages . . . and being married to two sisters at the same time . . . and the fact that they are both your first cousins—all of which, of course, is quite a boat load of things to forget. But let's try. Let's ask ourselves instead, what about Leah and her feelings? Did she feel like the ugly, unwanted sibling, second best, the one who always knew her husband preferred her younger sister? Did Jacob resent her or reject her? Apparently Jacob and Leah made the best of the situation. In fact, it seems that they got along pretty well, especially when we read in Genesis that she gave birth to four sons with Jacob. Far from being unhappy or resentful, apparently they were somewhat chummy.

On the occasion of the birth of their fourth son, Leah made three statements that are important to remember if we are or ever hope to be in a serious relationship—whether that is a marriage, a long-term romance, a family relationship, or a friendship. Leah made statements that revealed what people who love us and need us desire from us.

She wanted Jacob to love her. "And Leah conceived and bore a son, and she called his name Reuben; for she said, 'Because the LORD has looked upon my affliction; surely now my husband will love me.'"

Years ago when Page and I were dating and beginning to think that maybe we could have a future together, I asked her, "What do you want in a husband?" Thank God she didn't say she wanted someone who is stunningly handsome or handy enough to know a screwdriver from a hammer.

Instead, she said, "I want a good man who loves me." Isn't that what we want from relationships (whether they are romances or friendships)? We want the other person to be good—to be honest and trustworthy and kind, *and* we want to know they love us. If we want that from others, that is also what they want from us. Leo Buscaglia was right when he said, "Find love, find life." What did Leah want from Jacob? She wanted a good man who loved her.

She wanted Jacob to commit to her. "Again she conceived and bore a son, and said, 'Now this time my husband will be joined to me, because I have borne him three sons.'"

"My husband will be joined to me" is a phrase that goes past loving and includes commitment. The conductor of a community orchestra was trying to prepare his volunteer musicians for the annual Fourth of July Concert in the Park. Doing so was almost driving him out of his mind. At every single rehearsal, there had been at least one member missing, and usually it was several. Thus it became next to impossible for him to adequately prepare for the important event, as he had no idea how all the instruments would sound when blended together. At the last rehearsal, the night before the concert, he called for attention and said, "I would like to thank the first violinist for being the only member of the orchestra to attend every rehearsal." The violinist smiled shyly and humbly said to the conductor, "Well, it was the least I could do since I can't make it to the concert tomorrow."

Commitments are more than mere words, more than mere documents, more than mere legal arrangements. When someone loves us, we want to believe that we are special, that we can count on them, and that they will be there for us when we need them. And they need to believe the same about us. Leah wanted Jacob to commit to her.

She wanted Jacob to treat her with respect. In Genesis 30, Leah makes the statement, "Now, the other women will call me happy."

Why? Leah was pleased because when her sister, Rachel, had been infuriated over a personal issue and had vented her anger at her older sibling, Jacob had defended Leah. He stood up for her and showed her respect. "Now, the other women will call me happy."

Years ago, a staff member in a church I was serving saw every glass half empty and often told everyone else on staff why their ideas wouldn't work. She had a chip on her shoulder the size of New Hampshire. But she handled several of her responsibilities well. She related positively to most members of the congregation. She had small children at home who needed her income. And she had a certain constituency in the church that I didn't want to upset. So I labored with how to deal with her and finally decided to manage by avoiding. I would go my way and let her go hers. I simply avoided her as much as humanly possible. It worked for a while (at least, from my point of view), but then came the day when she went out of her way to create a conflict with me. The issue she chose had nothing to do with her responsibilities. It was totally in my portfolio. I said to her, "I am your supervisor, and I do not choose to argue with you." She answered, "I don't want to argue with you. I just don't want to be invisible anymore!" Suddenly I got it. To her, the distance I had created between us felt like dismissal. All she was asking for was my respect. From that moment on I tried to offer that to her, and she did to me. We still never saw eye to eye on a lot of things, but we learned to coexist. Occasionally we chatted and sometimes laughed and no longer felt so stressed around one another, simply because we decided to be respectful.

Sometimes showing respect is as simple as asking someone's opinion, whether you're interested in it or not; taking a moment to compliment a person on a task well done, however small, or listening to someone with patience, as if you care about what he or she has to say. Usually, if we show respect to others, they will give the same thing back to us. And even on the rare occasion when that doesn't happen, we will still be able to respect ourselves for how we treat people.

The story of Leah tells us three things that we desire from others and they desire from us, three things that are fundamental to happy, healthy, lasting relationships:

- We want people to *love* us.
- We want people to *commit* to us.
- We want people to *respect* us.

When those are the blocks we use as a foundation for our relationships, the houses we build will stand.

Reflection

1. What do you personally expect (and need) from someone you love?

_____

_____

_____

_____

2. How can people make behavioral covenants to increase the likelihood of lasting, healthy relationships? Are such covenants reasonable? Will they add to or restrict natural relating between individuals?

_____

_____

_____

_____

3. Aside from the story of Leah and Jacob, name other biblical accounts of relationships that were healthy. What made them so?

_____

_____

_____

_____

Facing Fundamentalism

Seeing the crowds, he went up on the mountain, and when he sat down his disciples came to him. And he opened his mouth and taught them, saying:

"Blessed are the poor in spirit, for theirs is the kingdom of heaven. Blessed are those who mourn, for they shall be comforted. Blessed are the meek, for they shall inherit the earth. Blessed are those who hunger and thirst for righteousness, for they shall be satisfied. Blessed are the merciful, for they shall obtain mercy. Blessed are the pure in heart, for they shall see God. Blessed are the peacemakers, for they shall be called sons of God. Blessed are those who are persecuted for righteousness' sake, for theirs is the kingdom of heaven. Blessed are you when men revile you and persecute you and utter all kinds of evil against you falsely on my account. Rejoice and be glad, for your reward is great in heaven, for so men persecuted the prophets who were before you." (Matthew 5:1-11)

Recently one of my staff members gave me an Internet list of suggested bumper-sticker mottos for each of the fifty states. All are tongue-in-cheek. Consider a few of the suggestions on the list. I will not identify them by the names of the states that appeared in the article, but they are amusing enough on their own:

- "If you can dream it, we can tax it."
- "Hey! It's dry heat."
- "We like chemicals in our water."
- "Spotted owl—It tastes just like chicken."

• And for one of the Great Lakes states, "Your first line of defense against Canadian invasion."

One of my favorites, from yet another state that I will leave unnamed in case a reader happens to live there, was the suggested motto, "We put the 'Fun' back into Fundamentalism."

There is, has always been, and, one suspects, will always be a debate regarding religious fundamentalism, and it is anything but "fun." Unthinkable acts of cruelty appear in the daily news committed by religious extremists (fundamentalists) who do ungodly things in the name of God. Whether you are Christian, Jewish, Muslim, or a practitioner of any other religious faith, there is real danger associated with thinking that one has all the answers, that one's position is the only position, and that God is for us and against all the others. Such unenlightened and unfaithful thinking, all in the name of faith, goes against every reasonable understanding of who God is and what God desires of us.

In the Christian faith, we know what the debate feels like. There are certain litmus-test questions:

• "Do you believe in the literal interpretation of the Bible?"
• "Do you believe in the literal interpretation of the Virgin Birth?"
• "Do you believe in the literal reality of hell?"
• "Do you believe that Revelation is prophetic as opposed to apocalyptic?"

If you do not answer Yes to each of those questions, then some will say that you are not "fundamentally" a Christian. The debate rages on between those who view the Bible as literal and those who view it as inspired, between those who see Christianity as a dogmatic system and those who see it as a journey of faith and discipleship.

When Jesus taught what it fundamentally means to be a believer, he did not talk much about some of the issues we think are front and center. Instead, he talked about one's spirit. He talked about one's perspective. He talked about one's commitments. He talked about how one treats other people. He talked about love. Read the Beatitudes (Matt 5:1-12). It's all there. "Blessed are the meek, the merciful, the pure in heart, the peacemakers, [even] those who are persecuted because in their daily behavior they do the right thing." He did not describe people who are rigidly committed to non-negotiable dogmatic statements. He described, instead, people who are motivated in all places at all times by a spirit of uncompromised love.

That's it. He indicated that fundamentally our faith is all about loving—believing that God loves us and then doing our best to live up to that love by passing it along to others. When the topic is fundamentals, Jesus said it all boils down to love. Purity. Mercy. Peacemaking. Doing the right thing to everyone, even if we have to pay a price because of it.

A high school girl found a love note taped to her locker at school. It was from her new boyfriend. The two of them had a date planned for the coming Sunday. Something of an underachiever, he had no car or income but intended to walk to her house and bring along a movie on DVD. Taped to her locker was this passionate note, "For you I would cross the hottest desert. For you I would swim the deepest sea. For you I would climb the highest mountain. I love you. I love you. I love you. P.S. I'll see you Sunday if it doesn't rain." It's the story of someone who proclaimed the principles of romance but missed the fundamentals.

Jesus was often chastised by fundamentalists who missed the fundamentals. The Pharisees were consistently uptight about rules and regulations. They condemned Jesus—finally even to a cross—because he didn't share their kind of fundamentalism. They said they had fulfilled their obligation to God by paying their tithes, which is a wonderful thing (and every pastor would love to have a few more people who follow that example), but Jesus said that at the same time they were allowing their aged parents to go hungry. They said that the Law was paramount and that anyone who broke it should be stoned to death, but Jesus believed in grace, fresh starts, and second chances, and so he said to the woman whom they were about to kill, "Your sins are forgiven; go your way, and do not sin like this again." They believed it was wrong to work on the Sabbath, but Jesus placed people above ritual. So, on the Sabbath, he healed a paralytic man and restored sight to another who could not see. "The Sabbath is made for people," he rightly observed, "and not people for the Sabbath." And of course, the Pharisees condemned him for it.

Many of the Pharisees were so bound by rules that there was no room for love, so committed to a strict interpretation of the "Thou shalts" and "Thou shalt nots" that grace, compassion, and charity were foreign concepts to them. They were religious fundamentalists whose extremism made them almost sacrilegious. We are not unfamiliar with that concept. In the present age, it is hard to turn on the evening news without seeing heart-rending illustrations of modern-day, and often deadly, Pharisaism. Considering all that the Messiah said and still says, if you want to talk fundamentals, it all boils down to love. It all boils down to a purity of heart, a meekness of spirit, that is merciful, peaceful, and so hungry and thirsty for right living and right relationships that it will risk even personal persecution in order to keep love alive in the world. Do we want to talk fundamentalism? According to Jesus, fundamentally the entire Christian faith is always about love.

Someone shared with me a story he attributed to a woman named LaVonn Steiner. She told of her daddy's hardware store in Mott, North Dakota, a small town on the prairies. One year on Christmas Eve, she was helping in her dad's store when a little boy, no more than five or six years old, came in. He was wearing a brown tattered coat with dirty, worn clothes beneath it. When he pulled off his cap, she saw that his hair was in disarray with cowlicks reminiscent of Alfalfa or Dennis the Menace. His shoes were scuffed, and only one had a lace. If a person were only minimally observant, it was easy to see that he was a child of poverty. He browsed around the small toy section of the family hardware store, picked up several items, examined them one by one, and then carefully put them back on the shelf. Ms. Steiner said that her dad walked over to the child, as respectfully as he would to any other customer, and asked if he could help. The little boy said, "I'm looking for a gift for my brother." Her dad told the child to make himself at home. After about twenty minutes, the child picked up a carved toy airplane. He cradled it in his hands as if it were made of crystal and carried it to LaVonn's father. "How much is this?" he asked. "My brother loves airplanes."

Her dad answered, "How much money do you have?"

The little boy reached into his tattered coat and pulled out a handful of change. He spread his money on the counter and began to count. "I have twenty-seven cents," he announced.

Her dad picked up the coins, and announced, "Isn't that something? That airplane cost exactly twenty-seven cents! Wait here, and I'll have it wrapped for you." Her father then put the toy into a box and wrapped it with paper and a big bow, and the child exited the store with a smile of total satisfaction. LaVonn made her way back to the toy section where she found the plane's shipping box under the counter. Checking the tag, she saw that it was priced to sell at $11.98. She never mentioned it to her father, nor did he say anything more about it to her, but she noted later, "My best gift that Christmas was seeing my dad's love in action."

I don't know what church LaVonn Steiner's father belongs to, or if he belongs to one at all, but I do know that what she saw him do on that cold December day in North Dakota was fundamentally Christian. It was love in action. And that is what Jesus calls believers to do when the fine points of theology have been debated and put away. "This is my commandment, that you love one another" (John 13:34). The New Testament's definition of "fundamentalism" is never an articulation of rigid rules or intractable dogmas. The New Testament teaches that when we put Christlike love into action, we are fundamentally Christian.

Jesus told his followers, of course, that love is not always an easy path to walk. He challenged them to "love your enemies, and pray for those who despitefully use you" (Matt 5:34). Authentic Christian fundamentalism calls us not merely to love but also to love people who are not easy to love, people who don't have the money to pay for the toy plane, people who do not live up to stated expectations, people who disappoint us or use us or refuse to love us even when we try to love them. Christlike love, *agape*, is unconditional. We love imperfect people, people who do not keep all the rules, people who don't deserve it. We do that because in similar fashion God loves us in spite of our own imperfections. W. H. Auden captured the meaning of unconditional love with these words:

O stand, stand in the window
As the tears scald and start.
You shall love your crooked neighbor
With all your crooked heart.[14]

Sam Keen wrote a wonderful book titled *To Love and Be Loved*. In it he talks about Christian *agape*. "*Agape* . . . is the capacity to love worthless people . . . [to say] You exist, therefore you are worthy of loving!"[15]

Fundamental Christianity does not give you and me the opportunity to choose whom we shall love and whom we shall hate, whom we shall nurture and whom we shall dismiss. Fundamental Christianity simply says, for better or worse, "You exist, therefore you are worthy of loving!"

That is what "fundamentalism" means in the best and purest sense of the word. Biblically, it all boils down to love—love for God and love for people, sometimes even when people don't make loving easy. That's what Jesus meant by meekness (which is not a synonym for weakness), purity of heart, a hunger and thirst for right living, and mercy. That's what he meant when he said, "Blessed are the peacemakers."

In the Ken Burns PBS series *The Civil War*, there were a number of scenes of the fiftieth anniversary of the Battle of Gettysburg. The anniversary was in 1913. A group of old Union and Confederate veterans returned to commemorate the occasion. Rare photos show the men talking over old times, sharing stories, and eating together. Then came a reenactment of Pickett's charge. Onlookers reported what happened next (supported by photos Burns included). Aging Union soldiers took their places, as they had fifty years earlier, among the rocks on Seminary Ridge. The old Confederate soldiers took their places on the farmland below. After a while, the Confederate soldiers started to move forward across the broad, flat field where just fifty years earlier so many had died. "We could not see rifles and bayonets," an eyewitness said, "but instead canes and crutches," as men no longer young made their slow advance toward the ridge. When the Confederate veterans got near the Union line, they broke into a long rebel yell. That was when the most fascinating thing happened. Unable to restrain themselves any longer, the Union troops burst out from behind the stone wall and flung themselves upon their former enemies. Only this time, the men in blue and the men in gray did not fight. Instead, they threw their arms around one another and stood and held on and wept. What a difference fifty years had made. In that moment, they understood that in the end we are all family with one another. We are created not to do battle but simply to love.

What is the bottom line for people of faith? What is Christianity fundamentally about? When the debates and arguments are over, it all comes down to this: "Blessed are the poor in spirit, blessed are the meek, blessed are those who hunger and thirst for righteousness, blessed are the merciful, blessed are the pure in heart, blessed are the peacemakers, blessed are those who are committed to living in right ways and treating all people with dignity, kindness, and compassion, no matter what the risks . . . for all of them are part of the kingdom of heaven." Or, to reduce that to the central dictate of Scripture, "This is my commandment, that you love one another."

Reflection

1. The argument has been made that Jesus offended the religious hierarchy of his day because he called for a return to fundamental Hebraic faith and practice. To what extent do you agree or disagree with that statement? If there is validity to it, what do you think were the fundamentals that Jesus seemed to consider non-negotiable?

_____

_____

_____

_____

2. Consider national or global examples of fundamental religious commitments that help enhance human life, and religious extremism that diminishes human life.

_____

_____

_____

_____

3. What are the bottom-line fundamentals of faith to which you are committed?

_____

_____

_____

_____

Choosing to Be a Christian

"When the Son of Man comes in his glory, and all the angels with him, then he will sit on his glorious throne. Before him will be gathered all the nations, and he will separate them one from another as a shepherd separates the sheep from the goats, and he will place the sheep at his right hand, but the goats at the left. Then the King will say to those at his right hand, 'Come, O blessed of my Father, inherit the kingdom prepared for you from the foundation of the world; for I was hungry and you gave me food, I was thirsty and you gave me drink, I was a stranger and you welcomed me, I was naked and you clothed me, I was sick and you visited me, I was in prison and you came to me.' Then the righteous will answer him, 'Lord, when did we see thee hungry and feed thee, or thirsty and give thee drink? And when did we see thee a stranger and welcome thee, or naked and clothe thee? And when did we see thee sick or in prison and visit thee?' And the King will answer them, 'Truly, I say to you, as you did it to one of the least of these my brethren, you did it to me.' Then he will say to those at his left hand, 'Depart from me, you cursed, into the eternal fire prepared for the devil and his angels; for I was hungry and you gave me no food, I was thirsty and you gave me no drink, I was a stranger and you did not welcome me, naked and you did not clothe me, sick and in prison and you did not visit me.' Then they also will answer, 'Lord, when did we see thee hungry or thirsty or a stranger or naked or sick or in prison, and did not minister to thee?' Then he will answer them, 'Truly, I say to you, as you did it not to one of the least of these, you did it not to me.'" (Matthew 25:31-45)

A friend commented to me that he finds it intriguing that the happiest season of the year is immediately preceded by what many Christians consider to be the most difficult day. The happiest season, he feels, is Advent (leading up to Christmas). I get that. The Advent/Christmas message is warm and fuzzy—thinking of the gift of a Messiah *to* us. But the Sunday in the Church Year immediately before Advent is Christ the King Sunday. It's not as warm and fuzzy because it forces us to think about the demands of a Lord *on* us. "Unto us a Child is born, unto us a Son is given." "Unto you is born this day in the City of David a Savior." Who doesn't feel good about texts like those? But, just as we are not allowed to jump past the cross to get to the resurrection, neither are we allowed to jump past the Lordship of Jesus to get to the Messiahship of Jesus. It is both logically and theologically impossible to accept as gracious Savior the same One whom we reject as Lord and King. Still, whether or not that is profoundly illogical, we keep trying.

A staff member of mine tells the story of bumping into a woman waiting for an elevator in a crowded New York lobby. My staff member recognized the woman and greeted her. After a moment's pleasantries, the staffer said, "You used to be so active at our church. Then all of a sudden, you just disappeared. What happened?" The woman answered, "I got better." Is that what faith is about? "I got better"? There was no acknowledgment that we are blessed to be blessings, that we are healed to be healers, or, as Bill Easum says, that "God's love always comes to us on its way to somebody else." Her words represented a consumer mentality. "What's in it for me? What have you done lately, God, and what can you still do to make my life in this world better?"

And those sentiments are not limited to "this world." Sometimes we embrace faith like a spiritual insurance policy. Believe in Jesus, take on his name, and when we die he will take us to heaven. I love all sorts of church music. Having grown up in the South, I enjoy the beats and beautiful harmonies of Southern Gospel songs. All the beats and harmonies notwithstanding, however, I have noticed that the theme of most songs in the genre is the same. It's all about where we go when die. You don't hear a lot of lyrics about discipleship, "Take up your cross and follow," servant leadership, or justice. Instead, it's all about the next world and rarely about the fact that maybe Christ the King calls me to create a little bit of heaven amid the hellishness of this world. Years ago I heard Gilbert Caldwell say, "Some people are so heavenly bound that they are no earthly good." However hard we try, it is impossible to accept as Messiah the same One whom we reject as Lord or King.

My grandmother used to say, "For a Christian, there's no wall between believing and behaving!" Jesus agreed with that. Consider his parable from Matthew 25. We should always read it, I think, alongside a similar story

Jesus tells earlier in the Gospel. In Matthew 7, he talks about how people approach the throne of judgment with confidence, pride, almost arrogance. They virtually swagger up to the Judge, very much full of themselves, and say "Did we not say, 'Lord, Lord'?" "Did we not sing the songs and pray the prayers and preach the sermons? Did we not talk a good game about our faith?" And basically the Judge answers, "Talk is cheap!" "Depart from me . . . for I was hungry, thirsty, sick, imprisoned, naked, a stranger in your midst, and you never lifted a finger to help me." And how do they answer? "But, Lord, if we had known it was you . . . ." The Judge replies, "What difference does it make who you thought it was? For when you failed to love one of the least of these, my brothers and sisters, you failed to love me! And vice versa, when you extended kindness to one of the least of these, you did so likewise unto me." Jesus was clear in saying that we cannot accept as Christ the Messiah the same One whom we reject as Christ the King.

Here's the issue that confronts us sooner or later: *if I call myself a "Christian," am I prepared to live like one?* At some point as disciples, there's no avoiding that question because, at a fundamental level, Christianity is a choice we make. Am I willing to follow where Christ leads? And before we step forward too quickly to say, "Lord, Lord," "Ride On, King Jesus," "Where He Leads Me, I Will Follow," let's at least be honest enough to confess that sometimes Jesus leads us to places we don't want to go! Remember some of the stuff this "King of kings" requests of us.

• "Sell what you possess, and give to the poor." (Hungry kids upset me as much as anyone else. But I've got bills to pay, and I promised my family a trip to Aruba. Anyway, surely there are jobs out there for "those people," right?)
• "Love your enemies, and pray for those who despitefully use you." (My enemies? All my enemies? There have to be codicils, right? I mean, I can't be expected to pray for Putin or Assad or my nasty-natured boss at work or the professor who gave me a D or the student who gave me an ulcer or an ex-spouse who was abusive or unfaithful.)
• "Render unto God what is God's." (But everything is God's. So does that mean I would have to give God a role in what I do with everything? My money, my time, my relationships, how I vote, how I manage my business, what I say to people or about people, the whole nine yards? I don't think so.)

• "Go back to the Decapolis, sharing with all what the Lord has done for you." (Oh, please. We've got to hit the "Delete" button on that one. I mean, Lord, you have no idea how people look at me over the water cooler or at the fitness center or in the dorm if I talk about my faith. You'd think I was from Jupiter or Mars!)

• "Turn the other cheek." (Yeah, right! The last time I tried it, that cheek got slapped, too!)

• "This is my commandment, that you love one another." (Maybe if people would try to see things my way once in a while, try to be a little more flexible, a little more accommodating . . . . Really, it's their fault for not being lovable!)

Choosing to be a Christian, choosing to follow Christ, means choosing to live according to statements like those—not just to say "Lord, Lord," not just to sing "Oh, How I Love Jesus," but to follow where Jesus leads, even if he leads us places we do not want to go.

The minister who confirmed me into the Methodist church at age twelve was one of the dearest, gentlest human beings I ever knew. He and my father were close friends. After the pastor died, my dad told me a story about him. He confessed to my dad that he had grown up in an abusive home. After his mother died, his father remarried. The new wife could easily have been the wicked stepmother from *Cinderella*. She resented him and abused him both verbally and physically. Sometimes she would slap him and then lock him in the backyard, threatening to leave him there all night even if the weather were cold or rainy. He was just a little boy in elementary school. He would bang on the door, crying, begging to come in, promising not to disappoint her anymore, and apologizing for something (though he had no idea what it was). Sometimes after an hour or two, she would let him. But other times the lights would go out, and the door would remain locked. On those occasions, he would curl up on the doormat like a pet dog, shivering and crying himself to sleep. The next morning, she would open the door and say, "Get dressed for school. There's no time for breakfast. You better not be late!"

That was how he grew up. And yet somehow he still became a good student, a fine athlete, and a well-educated young man with a bachelor's and a master's degree. In fact, he went on to become a successful Methodist pastor with a distinguished career. In his stepmother's later years, when she was confined to bed due to a debilitating illness, her biological children basically deserted her, had nothing to do with her, and took no responsibility for her. So that pastor, the one she had locked in the back-yard, unlocked his home to her. He took her in and looked after her with compassion and kindness. He treated her as if she had been the best mom imaginable, literally until the day she died under his roof. My dad said to him, "I can't believe you did that for her after how she treated you." He answered, "I didn't just do it for her. I also did it for myself. For one, the burden of anger was too heavy to bear. It would've taken all the joy out of my life. But even more," he said, "I figured if I cannot love people who make loving difficult, how could I ever stand in a pulpit and preach about love to anyone else?" He got it. He understood. He didn't just talk about following Jesus; he actually rose up and followed.

"Did we not say, 'Lord, Lord'?" they asked. And Jesus answered that Christianity is not merely a faith you profess. It is a choice you make about how you will do your living in the world. It really is about "walking the walk," about following where Jesus leads, living as Jesus lived, and loving as Jesus loved even when it would be easier not to.

Are we serious about doing that, even if stretches us, which it will? Are we serious about taking the Christian faith out of the chapel into the office, the dorm, the home, the neighborhood, the voting booth, the avenues where people encounter other people every day in the world? Because if Jesus is not "King of kings" for me in all those places, then even in the glorious setting of a beautiful sanctuary it probably doesn't matter much. If we do not seek to serve him, however difficult that may be, out in the world, then what we do in church may well be religious but ultimately irrelevant. For Christians, sooner or later it all boils down to this: as my grandmother said, there is no wall between believing and behaving, between grace and discipleship, between accepting Christ the Messiah and following Christ the King.

Reflection

1. What is the difference between grace and discipleship?

_____

_____

_____

_____

2. What is the difference between pride and a sense of self-worth?

_____

_____

_____

_____

3. Name three things God asks of churches and three things God asks of individuals that they might be reluctant to do. Why?

_____

_____

_____

_____

Simply Loving

And one of the scribes came up and heard them disputing with one another, and seeing that he answered them well, asked him, "Which commandment is the first of all?" Jesus answered, "The first is, 'Hear, O Israel: The Lord our God, the Lord is one; and you shall love the Lord your God with all your heart, and with all your soul, and with all your mind, and with all your strength.' The second is this, 'You shall love your neighbor as yourself.' There is no other commandment greater than these." And the scribe said to him, "You are right, Teacher; you have truly said that he is one, and there is no other but he; and to love him with all the heart, and with all the understanding, and with all the strength, and to love one's neighbor as oneself, is much more than all whole burnt offerings and sacrifices." And when Jesus saw that he answered wisely, he said to him, "You are not far from the kingdom of God." And after that no one dared to ask him any question. (Mark 12:28-34)

A five-year-old walked into the den where his dad was reading the paper. In a straightforward way, the child asked, "Daddy, where did I come from?" The father gulped. Thinking that this inevitable question had come a bit sooner than he expected or desired it would, he nonetheless decided that if this child asked an honest question, he deserved an honest answer. And so, delicately but honestly, the father walked his five-year-old son through the entire story of the birds and the bees. The whole while, the child just stood there, saying nothing. Finally he turned and walked into the kitchen. His father heard the little boy say to his mom, "Mommy, where did I come from?" The mother answered, "Baltimore," to which her son said, "Thanks, Mommy. I asked Daddy, but he didn't have a clue!"

Sometimes, albeit from well-meaning motives, we complicate things far more than we need to.

Karl Barth was perhaps America's premier theologian of the twentieth century, a man who helped articulate neo-orthodoxy in a way that had not been communicated since the days of Luther. Barth's *Dogmatics* is still required reading, as well it should be, in most seminaries. That work spells out the particulars of Christian doctrine more powerfully than any book since the Bible itself. Barth was nothing short of a theological genius.

The story is told that Dr. Barth was invited to lecture at the Theological School of the University of Chicago, one of the finest and most scholarly seminaries in the nation. Barth's message that night was predictably brilliant and deep. Afterward, there was a time for Q and A. A young student, working on his PhD, asked, "Dr. Barth, can you state for us the central thesis of the Christian faith?" Everyone expected something so cerebral that they would have to access their dictionaries to interpret the language, let alone to grasp the concepts. Instead, Karl Barth took a deep breath and answered, "As I see it, the central thesis of the Christian faith is this: Jesus loves me, this I know, for the Bible tells me so." When all the scholarship had been explored and exhausted, that great theologian returned to the simplicity of it all. For Barth, as for the New Testament, the bottom line of the Christian faith was simply Love.

At the end of the day, most of us are looking for a simple, understandable word about life and faith. While theological exploration, biblical exegesis, and diligent study are indispensable for Christian growth, at some point we still long to hear it simply put.

That, to a great extent, explains the popularity of Billy Graham. He always understood his audience's need to hear faith clearly stated. That is one of the key reasons that he consistently attracted such massive crowds. His message was simple, clear, and easy to understand. Every time you heard him preach, the message was, "You must be born again." Dr. Graham himself says that basically he always preached the same sermon and simply changed the illustrations. The argument could be made that such is the reason behind the enormous popularity of Norman Vincent Peale, Robert Schuller, Joyce Meyer, and Joel Osteen as well. Running through each of their ministries was (and for Osteen and Meyer still is) a consistent thread that ties it all together, one ongoing theme that listeners can count on and understand.

"Simplicity," it is said, "is the queen of the virtues." Jesus, the greatest preacher of all the ages, would have agreed. No one ever possessed nor will ever possess the wisdom of Christ. The New Testament says, "In the beginning was the Logos [the mind of God] . . . and the mind of God became flesh and dwelt among us." In other words, Jesus had within himself the very wisdom of God. More than anyone else, he was infinitely capable of soaring above the heads of his listeners if he chose to do so. But when a scribe asked what faith and discipleship are all about, Jesus answered simply, "You shall love the Lord your God . . . and you shall love your neighbor as yourself." When everything else was said and done, Jesus taught that all our theologizing, all our theorizing, all our preaching, and all our wrestling with dogma and doctrine bring us to the same place. At the end, it all boils down to Love. That explains, I think, why the only time Jesus ever used any form of the word "command" was when he said, "This is my commandment, that you love one another."

Far too many buy into the myth that life is about money and possessions. Those who are truly wise know better. The simple truth is, you cannot take it with you. As the saying goes, "You have never seen a U-Haul at the rear of a hearse." Years ago a wealthy oil tycoon came to the end of his life. He lay in his bed in a mansion of almost indescribable opulence. He had all the things money can buy, but something vital had been missing throughout his life and was still missing at the conclusion. There were no friends or family members seated by his bed. Most of them were either jockeying for position back in the corporate headquarters or lobbying the family attorney to determine if they would be happy with the provisions of the will. A household servant brought the dying man a cup of tea. Taking the cup from the gentleman's hand, the man in the bed made the statement, "I would have traded all this to have been loved by someone." For a moment there was only silence. Then he continued, "Maybe if I had made more investments in loving across the years, I would be receiving more dividends at the end."

It is not our accumulations or possessions that make life livable. Money is no more than a paper symbol, reminding us of what we can do or choose not to do to make the world a better place. It cannot be taken with us, nor can it ultimately become a source of meaning, peace, or satisfaction.

The same holds true, of course, with prestige and power. Mother Teresa had prestige, but so did Jesse James. Albert Schweitzer had prestige, but so did Osama bin Laden. Life is about something other than that, as Mother Theresa and Dr. Schweitzer understood and demonstrated in their living.

Jesus said that what matters most is not always what we give our time or efforts to. Instead, he said simply, here is what ultimately makes sense of life: "You shall love the Lord your God . . . and you shall love your neighbor as yourself." It's all about Love. That divine truth is wise, honest, and simple.

It is easy to fall into the trap of making life too complicated. Thus I have tried to develop a simple *credo* to live by. It is not exhaustive, and I don't know whether it sounds more like Jesus or Robert Fulghum. Either way, here's a simple list of things I try to keep in mind that helps me navigate the floodwaters of life. They are my own simple truths to live by:

• Love is stronger than hate.
• Faith is better than fear.
• Smiles and tears are both important, and we should not be embarrassed by either.
• Grief hurts. Don't deny it.
• Most people are better than we give them credit for being.
• Having a large balance in your bank account is not as meaningful as having people who want to go to lunch with you tomorrow or people who want you to come home to them this afternoon.
• If you don't allow yourself productive quiet times, you'll never have much of worth to say when it is time for conversation.
• Not everyone will like you. Get over it.
• Children are as close to being angels as anything we are ever going to see on this earth.
• If you make the decision simply to do one good deed every day, your life will make the earth a different place.
• If you cannot say, "I love you," you are missing a source of deep joy.
• If you cannot show love, you are missing the meaning of life.

This list of random thoughts is my personal formula for making sense of life. Its fabric is woven with a word that is divinely clear and comprehensible. "What is life all about?" Jesus was asked. And he answered, "You shall love the Lord your God . . . and you shall love your neighbor as yourself." It really is that simple.

Reflection

1. Jesus said, "You shall love your neighbor *as yourself.*" How, within the parameters of Christian discipleship, should one practice self-love?

_____

_____

_____

_____

2. Discuss or consider the meaning of these words from the epistle of 1 John: "You cannot love God, whom you have not seen, if you hate your brother or sister, whom you have seen" (4:20). Name specific ways of putting love into action, especially toward people who are difficult to love.

_____

_____

_____

_____

3. Write your personal *credo* for life.

_____

_____

_____

_____

Notes

1. Paula Gooder, *Everyday God: The Spirit of Ordinary Time* (London: Canterbury Press, 2012) 27.

2. Commonly attributed to English poet Frederick Langbridge.

3. Henri Nouwen, *Beloved* (London: Canterbury Press, 2007).

4. Catherine Marshall, *A Man Called Peter* (Grand Rapids MI: Baker Book House, re-published 2001).

5. William Cullen Bryant, "Ode to a Waterfowl," in Bliss Perry, ed., *The American Spirit In Literature: A Chronicle Of Great Interpreters* (New Haven CT: Yale University Press, 1918).

6. Harold Kushner, *When Bad Things Happen to Good People* (New York: Anchor Books, 2004).

7. Robert Browning Hamilton, "Along the Road," in Hazel Felleman, ed., *The Best Loved Poems of American People* (New York: Doubleday Publishing, 2008).

8. Dan Schutte, "Here I Am, Lord," *The United Methodist Hymnal* (Nashville: The United Methodist Publishing House, 1989) 593–94.

9. Bryant M. Kirkland, *Living in a Zigzag Age* (Nashville: Abingdon Press, 1972) 76.

10. Original source unknown (but sometimes attributed to Ralph Waldo Emerson as the saying may be a variation of "life is a progress, and not a station," from Emerson's "Compensation," in *Prose Works of Ralph Waldo Emerson*, vol. 1 [Boston: James R. Osgood and Co., 1875] 279).

11. Ron Newhouse, from www.devotions.net, his website that offers one devotion each day. (No archives available.)

12. Richard B. Wilke, *And Are We Yet Alive?* (Nashville: Abingdon Press, 1986) 124.

13. Maxwell Perkins, quoted by Father Henry Fehren in *U.S. Catholic* (May 1986).

14. W. H. Auden, "One Evening," from *W. H. Auden's Poems* (New York: Everyman's Library, 1995).

15. Sam Keen, *To Love and Be Loved* (New York: Bantam Press, 1999).

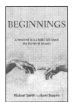

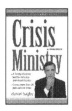

Crisis Ministry: A Handbook
Daniel G. Bagby

Covering more than 25 crisis pastoral care situations, this book provides a brief, practical guide for church leaders and other caregivers responding to stressful situations in the lives of parishioners. It tells how to resource caregiving professionals in the community who can help people in distress. *978-1-57312-370-9 154 pages/pb* **$15.00**

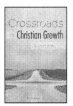

Crossroads in Christian Growth
W. Loyd Allen

Authentic Christian life presents spiritual crises and we struggle to find a hero walking with God at a crossroads. With wisdom and sincerity, W. Loyd Allen presents Jesus as our example and these crises as stages in the journey of growth we each take toward maturity in Christ. *978-1-57312-753-0 164 pages/pb* **$15.00**

A Divine Duet
Ministry and Motherhood
Alicia Davis Porterfield, ed.

Each essay in this inspiring collection is as different as the mother-minister who wrote it, from theologians to chaplains, inner-city ministers to rural-poverty ministers, youth pastors to preachers, mothers who have adopted, birthed, and done both. *978-1-57312-676-2 146 pages/pb* **$16.00**

The Exile and Beyond (All the Bible series)
Wayne Ballard

The Exile and Beyond brings to life the sacred literature of Israel and Judah that comprises the exilic and postexilic communities of faith. It covers Ezekiel, Isaiah, Haggai, Zechariah, Malachi, 1 & 2 Chronicles, Ezra, Nehemiah, Joel, Jonah, Song of Songs, Esther, and Daniel. *978-1-57312-759-2 196 pages/pb* **$16.00**

Fierce Love
Desperate Measures for Desperate Times
Jeanie Miley

Fierce Love is about learning to see yourself and know yourself as a conduit of love, operating from a full heart instead of trying to find someone to whom you can hook up your emotional hose and fill up your empty heart. *978-1-57312-810-0 276 pages/pb* **$18.00**

Five Hundred Miles
Reflections on Calling and Pilgrimage
Lauren Brewer Bass

Spain's Camino de Santiago, the Way of St. James, has been a cherished pilgrimage path for centuries, visited by countless people searching for healing, solace, purpose, and hope. These stories from her five-hundred-mile-walk is Lauren Brewer Bass's honest look at the often winding, always surprising journey of a calling.   *978-1-57312-812-4 142 pages/pb* **$16.00**

Galatians (Smyth & Helwys Bible Commentary)
Marion L. Soards and Darrell J. Pursiful

In Galatians, Paul endeavored to prevent the Gentile converts from embracing a version of the gospel that insisted on their observance of a form of the Mosaic Law. He saw with a unique clarity that such a message reduced the crucified Christ to being a mere agent of the Law. For Paul, the gospel of Jesus Christ alone, and him crucified, had no place in it for the claim that Law-observance was necessary for believers to experience the power of God's grace.   *978-1-57312-771-4 384 pages/hc* **$55.00**

Glimpses from State Street
Wayne Ballard

As a collection of devotionals, *Glimpses from State Street* provides a wealth of insights and new ways to consider and develop our fellowship with Christ. It also serves as a window into the relationship between a small town pastor and a welcoming congregation.

978-1-57312-841-4 158 pages/pb **$15.00**

God's Servants, the Prophets
Bryan Bibb

God's Servants, the Prophets covers the Israelite and Judean prophetic literature from the preexilic period. It includes Amos, Hosea, Isaiah, Micah, Zephaniah, Nahum, Habakkuk, Jeremiah, and Obadiah.

978-1-57312-758-5 208 pages/pb **$16.00**

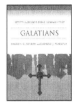

Gray Matters
100 Devotions for the Aging
Edwin Ray Frazier

"Each line rests on Frazier's fundamental belief that every season in life is valuable and rich with opportunity."

—Alicia Davis Porterfield
Interim pastor and former eldercare chaplain

978-1-57312-837-7 246 pages/pb **$18.00**

Hermeneutics of Hymnody
A Comprehensive and Integrated Approach to Understanding Hymns
Scotty Gray

Scotty Gray's *Hermeneutics of Hymnody* is a comprehensive and integrated approach to understanding hymns. It is unique in its holistic and interrelated exploration of seven of the broad facets of this most basic forms of Christian literature. A chapter is devoted to each and relates that facet to all of the others.   *978-157312-767-7 432 pages/pb* **$28.00**

If Jesus Isn't the Answer . . . He Sure Asks the Right Questions!
J. Daniel Day

Taking eleven of Jesus' questions as its core, Day invites readers into their own conversation with Jesus. Equal parts testimony, theological instruction, pastoral counseling, and autobiography, the book is ultimately an invitation to honest Christian discipleship.   *978-1-57312-797-4 148 pages/pb* **$16.00**

I'm Trying to Lead . . . Is Anybody Following?
The Challenge of Congregational Leadership in the Postmodern World
Charles B. Bugg

Bugg provides us with a view of leadership that has theological integrity, honors the diversity of church members, and reinforces the brave hearts of church leaders who offer vision and take risks in the service of Christ and the church.   *978-1-57312-731-8 136 pages/pb* **$13.00**

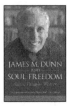

James M. Dunn and Soul Freedom
Aaron Douglas Weaver

James Milton Dunn, over the last fifty years, has been the most aggressive Baptist proponent for religious liberty in the US. Soul freedom—voluntary, uncoerced faith and an unfettered individual conscience before God—is the basis of his understanding of church-state separation and the historic Baptist basis of religious liberty.   *978-1-57312-590-1 224 pages/pb* **$18.00**

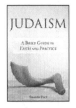

Judaism
A Brief Guide to Faith and Practice
Sharon Pace

Sharon Pace's newest book is a sensitive and comprehensive introduction to Judaism. How does belief in the One God and a universal morality shape the way in which Jews see the world? How does one find meaning in life and the courage to endure suffering? How does one mark joy and forge community ties?   *978-1-57312-644-1 144 pages/pb* **$16.00**

Luke (Smyth & Helwys Annual Bible Study series)
Parables for the Journey
Michael L. Ruffin

These stories in Luke's Gospel are pilgrimage parables. They are parables for those on the way to being the people of God. They are not places where we stop and stay; they are rather places where we learn what we need to learn and from which, equipped with Jesus' directions, we continue the journey. But we will see that they are also places to which we repeatedly return.
Teaching Guide 978-1-57312-849-0 146 pages/pb **$14.00**
Study Guide 978-1-57312-850-6 108 pages/pb **$6.00**

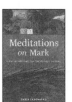

Meditations on Mark
Daily Devotions from the Oldest Gospel
Chris Cadenhead

Readers searching for a fresh encounter with Scripture can delve into *Meditations on Mark*, a collection of daily devotions intended to guide the reader through the book of Mark, the Oldest Gospel and the first known effort to summarize and proclaim the life and ministry of Jesus.
978-1-57312-851-3 158 pages/pb **$15.00**

Meeting Jesus Today
For the Cautious, the Curious, and the Committed
Jeanie Miley

Meeting Jesus Today, ideal for both individual study and small groups, is intended to be used as a workbook. It is designed to move readers from studying the Scriptures and ideas within the chapters to recording their journey with the Living Christ.
978-1-57312-677-9 320 pages/pb **$19.00**

The Ministry Life
101 Tips for New Ministers
John Killinger

Sharing years of wisdom from more than fifty years in ministry and teaching, *The Ministry Life: 101 Tips for New Ministers* by John Killinger is filled with practical advice and wisdom for a minister's day-to-day tasks as well as advice on intellectual and spiritual habits to keep ministers of any age healthy and fulfilled.
978-1-57312-662-5 244 pages/pb **$19.00**

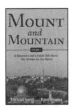

Mount and Mountain
Vol. 2: A Reverend and a Rabbi Talk About the Sermon on the Mount
Rami Shapiro and Michael Smith

This book, focused on the Sermon on the Mount, represents the second half of Mike and Rami's dialogue. In it, Mike and Rami explore the text of Jesus' sermon cooperatively, contributing perspectives drawn from their lives and religious traditions and seeking moments of illumination.
978-1-57312-654-0 254 pages/pb **$19.00**

Of Mice and Ministers
Musings and Conversations About Life, Death, Grace, and Everything
Bert Montgomery

With stories about pains, joys, and everyday life, *Of Mice and Ministers* finds Jesus in some unlikely places and challenges us to do the same. From tattooed women ministers to saying the "N"-word to the brotherly kiss, Bert Montgomery takes seriously the lesson from Psalm 139—where can one go that God is not already there?
978-1-57312-733-2 154 pages/pb **$14.00**

Place Value
The Journey to Where You Are
Katie Sciba

Does a place have value? Can a place change us? Is it possible for God to use the place you are in to form you? From Victoria, Texas to Indonesia, Belize, Australia, and beyond, Katie Sciba's wanderlust serves as a framework to understand your own places of deep emotion and how God may have been weaving redemption around you all along.
978-157312-829-2 138 pages/pb **$15.00**

Reading Joshua
(Reading the Old Testament series)
A Historical-Critical/Archaeological Commentary
John C. H. Laughlin

Using the best of current historical-critical studies by mainstream biblical scholars, and the most recent archaeological discoveries and theorizing, Laughlin questions both the historicity of the stories presented in the book as well as the basic theological ideology presented through these stories: namely that Yahweh ordered the indiscriminate butchery of the Canaanites.
978-1-57312-836-0 274 pages/pb **$32.00**

A Revolutionary Gospel
Salvation in the Theology of Walter Rauschenbusch
William Powell Tuck

William Powell Tuck describes how Rauschenbusch's concept of redemption requires a transformation of society as well as individuals—and that no one can genuinely be redeemed without this redemption affecting the social culture as well. A *Revolutionary Gospel* shows us how Rauschenbusch's revolutionary concept of salvation is still relevant today.

978-1-57312-804-9 190 pages/pb **$21.00**

Reflective Faith
A Theological Toolbox for Women
Susan M. Shaw

In *Reflective Faith*, Susan Shaw offers a set of tools to explore difficult issues of biblical interpretation, theology, church history, and ethics—especially as they relate to women. Reflective faith invites intellectual struggle and embraces the unknown; it is a way of discipleship, a way to love God with your mind, as well as your heart, your soul, and your strength.

978-1-57312-719-6 292 pages/pb **$24.00**
***Workbook** 978-1-57312-754-7 164 pages/pb* **$12.00**

Sessions with Ephesians
(Sessions Bible Studies series)
Toward a New Identity in Christ
William L. Self & Michael D. McCullar

Ephesians has been called "the most contemporary book in the Bible." Strip it of just a few first-century references and it would be easily applicable to the modern church.

978-1-57312-838-4 110 pages/pb **$14.00**

Sessions with Psalms (Sessions Bible Studies series)
Prayers for All Seasons
Eric and Alicia D. Porterfield

Useful to seminar leaders during preparation and group discussion, as well as in individual Bible study, *Sessions with Psalms* is a ten-session study designed to explore what it looks like for the words of the psalms to become the words of our prayers. Each session is followed by a thought-provoking page of questions.

978-1-57312-768-4 136 pages/pb **$14.00**

Tell the Truth, Shame the Devil
Stories about the Challenges of Young Pastors
James Elllis III, ed.

A pastor's life is uniquely difficult. *Tell the Truth, Shame the Devil*, then, is an attempt to expose some of the challenges that young clergy often face. While not exhaustive, this collection of essays is a superbly compelling and diverse introduction to how tough being a pastor under the age of thirty-five can be.   *978-1-57312-839-1 198 pages/pb* **$18.00**

Though the Darkness Gather Round
Devotions about Infertility, Miscarriage, and Infant Loss
Mary Elizabeth Hill Hanchey and Erin McClain, eds.

Much courage is required to weather the long grief of infertility and the sudden grief of miscarriage and infant loss. This collection of devotions by men and women, ministers, chaplains, and lay leaders who can speak of such sorrow, is a much-needed resource and precious gift for families on this journey and the faith communities that walk beside them.

978-1-57312-811-7 180 pages/pb **$19.00**

Time for Supper
Invitations to Christ's Table
Brett Younger

Some scholars suggest that every meal in literature is a communion scene. Could every meal in the Bible be a communion text? Could every passage be an invitation to God's grace? These meditations on the Lord's Supper help us listen to the myriad of ways God invites us to gratefully, reverently, and joyfully share the cup of Christ.   *978-1-57312-720-2 246 pages/pb* **$18.00**

A Time to Laugh
Humor in the Bible
Mark E. Biddle

With characteristic liveliness, Mark E. Biddle explores the ways humor was intentionally incorporated into Scripture. Drawing on Biddle's command of Hebrew language and cultural subtleties, *A Time to Laugh* guides the reader through the stories of six biblical characters who did rather unexpected things.   *978-1-57312-683-0 164 pages/pb* **$14.00**

A True Hope
Jedi Perils and the Way of Jesus
Joshua Hays

Star Wars offers an accessible starting point for considering substantive issues of faith, philosophy, and ethics. In *A True Hope*, Joshua Hays explores some of these challenging ideas through the sayings of the Jedi Masters, examining the ways the worldview of the Jedi is at odds with that of the Bible.   978-1-57312-770-7 *186 pages/pb* **$18.00**

Word of God Across the Ages
Using Christian History in Preaching
Bill J. Leonard

In this third, enlarged edition, Bill J. Leonard returns to the roots of the Christian story to find in the lives of our faithful forebears examples of the potent presence of the gospel. Through these stories, those who preach today will be challenged and inspired as they pursue the divine Word in human history through the ages.   978-1-57312-828-5 *174 pages/pb* **$19.00**

The World Is Waiting for You
Celebrating the 50th Ordination Anniversary of Addie Davis
Pamela R. Durso & LeAnn Gunter Johns, eds.

Hope for the church and the world is alive and well in the words of these gifted women. Keen insight, delightful observations, profound courage, and a gift for communicating the good news are woven throughout these sermons. The Spirit so evident in Addie's calling clearly continues in her legacy.   978-1-57312-732-5 *224 pages/pb* **$18.00**

With Us in the Wilderness
Finding God's Story in Our Lives
Laura A. Barclay

What stories compose your spiritual biography? In *With Us in the Wilderness*, Laura Barclay shares her own stories of the intersection of the divine and the everyday, guiding readers toward identifying and embracing God's presence in their own narratives.

978-1-57312-721-9 *120 pages/pb* **$13.00**